WARRIOR • 140

US MECHANIZED INFANTRYMAN IN THE FIRST GULF WAR

GORDON L ROTTMAN

ILLUSTRATED BY ADAM HOOK

Series editors Marcus Cowper and Nikolai Bogdanovic

First published in 2009 by Osprey Publishing
Midland House, West Way, Botley, Oxford OX2 0PH, UK
443 Park Avenue South, New York, NY 10016, USA

E-mail: info@ospreypublishing.com

ISBN: 978 1 84603 468 1
E-book ISBN: 978 1 84908 095 8

Editorial by Ilios Publishing Ltd, Oxford, UK (www.iliospublishing.com)
Design by PDQ Media
Index by Fineline Editorial Services
Originated by PDQ Media

09 10 11 12 13   10 9 8 7 6 5 4 3 2 1

A CIP catalog record for this book is available from the British Library.

Cover image: Infantrymen of the 2nd Bn, 41st Inf, 2nd Armored Div, exit an M2 Bradley IFV during a demonstration of a company team defense maneuver at the Antelope Mound training area. (Photo courtesy US DoD, photographer William Rosenmund)

ACKNOWLEDGMENTS

The author is indebted to Director Steve Draper of the 1st Cavalry Division Museum, Ft Hood, Texas, Archivist Grace Hardwick, and SSG Jimmy Stewart for their assistance. He also wishes to thank SFC Glen Bona for his insights on pre-Gulf War infantry training.

ARTIST'S NOTE

Readers may care to note that the original paintings from which the color plates in this book were prepared are available for private sale. All reproduction copyright whatsoever is retained by the Publishers. All enquiries should be addressed to:

Scorpio Gallery, PO Box 475, Hailsham, East Sussex, BN27 2SL, UK

The Publishers regret that they can enter into no correspondence upon this matter.

THE WOODLAND TRUST

Osprey Publishing are supporting the Woodland Trust, the UK's leading woodland conservation charity, by funding the dedication of trees.

FOR A CATALOGUE OF ALL BOOKS PUBLISHED BY OSPREY MILITARY AND AVIATION PLEASE CONTACT:

Osprey Direct, c/o Random House Distribution Center,
400 Hahn Road, Westminster, MD 21157
Email: uscustomerservice@ospreypublishing.com

Osprey Direct, The Book Service Ltd, Distribution Centre,
Colchester Road, Frating Green, Colchester, Essex, CO7 7DW
E-mail: customerservice@ospreypublishing.com

www.ospreypublishing.com

CONTENTS

US MECHANIZED INFANTRYMAN IN THE FIRST GULF WAR

INTRODUCTION

The 1990–91 Gulf War was the first true test of the modern US Army in the aftermath of Vietnam. While interventions had taken place in Grenada in 1983 and Panama in 1989, these were small-scale contingency operations of only a few days' duration involving special operations and light forces. This Army that fought the 1990–91 Gulf War had long prepared for Armageddon with the Soviet Union and the Warsaw Pact, as part of the Cold War army trained to face the Soviet juggernaut. It had also readied itself for a war in Korea and contingency operations any place in the world. As a result of its training and preparation for these missions it defeated the fourth largest army in the world in Operation *Desert Storm*.

After Vietnam the US Army underwent major changes in organization, structure, and philosophy. Universal Military Service – the draft – was eliminated in 1973 and the all-Volunteer Army (VOLAR) was instituted. Pay was increased, entry standards raised, and numerous incentives introduced ranging from education benefits, improved quarters, and the making of service life more appealing to families. Career opportunities were increased; generous reenlistment bonuses and non-commissioned officer (NCO) development improved with the promise of excellent retirement benefits. While there was no draft, 18-year-olds were required to register for a standby draft registration within 30 days of their birthday.

The Army was armed and equipped with some of the best weapons systems in the world, which had begun fielding just a few years previously. Many of these advanced and as yet unproved systems were controversial and criticized by the lay media. These included the M1 Abrams tank, M2 Bradley infantry fighting vehicle, and the multiple launch rocket system (MLRS). The same media were critical of the Army's ability to defeat a battle-hardened Iraqi Army, which had fought a long and brutal war with Iran. It made no difference that the US Army had been training long and hard to face the massive and well-armed armed forces of the Soviet Union.

A phrase often heard in the new army, with the recruiting motto of, "Be all you can be," was, "It's not your father's army." It really was not. Virtually every aspect of the Army had changed; not just uniforms, weapons, equipment, and pay, but its very fiber. The volunteer army suffered its growing pains through the 1970s as it changed and adapted. By the mid-1980s drug and race problems had been minimized. Women were integrated into the force structure after the Woman's Army Corps was dissolved in 1979, being assigned directly to non-combat arms units.

A major change had taken place in how training was conducted. Individual skills were taught in a method called "task, conditions, and standard" specifying what the task's mission or goal was, under what conditions and with what resources it was conducted, and the standards to be met. A soldier either passed or failed the test, a "go" or "no-go." Unit training was conducted in much the same manner, with units required to effectively accomplish a complex series of interrelated combat tasks simultaneously at multiple echelons, the Army Training and Evaluation Program.

Individual initial training changed too. Soldiers used to undertake eight weeks of Basic Combat Training (BCT) given to all soldiers regardless of their future assignment. This was followed, in the case of infantrymen, by eight weeks of Light Weapons Infantryman Advanced Individual Training (AIT). Infantrymen received one common program of instruction regardless of the type of unit they would be assigned to. BCT and AIT were conducted by different training units, often at different posts.

The new system was known as One-Station Unit Training (OSUT). A soldier was assigned to a training unit at Ft Benning, Georgia in the case of infantrymen, and remained with the same drill instructors through 13 weeks of specialized training either as a light infantryman (Military Occupation Specialty 11B) to be assigned to light, airborne, or air assault units or as a mechanized infantryman (MOS 11M) to be assigned to Bradley-equipped units. The Bradley was not just a "battle taxi," but a weapon system of which the squad was a part. In some ways the squad saw themselves more as a part of the crew rather than merely as a dismountable infantry element.

Besides its heavily armed rifle squad the Bradley M2 infantry fighting vehicle (IFV) mounted tremendous firepower, making it a lethal combat vehicle even without its squad: a 25mm automatic gun able to knock out lightly armored vehicles and fighting positions, a twin tube TOW antiarmor wire-guided missile launcher capable of defeating any tank in the world, a 7.62mm machine gun, and smoke grenade dischargers. (For further details, see Osprey New Vanguard 18, *The M2/M3 Bradley Infantry Fighting Vehicle 1983-95.*)

Iraq's illegal invasion of Kuwait on August 2, 1990 saw the immediate deployment of US and other nations' units to Saudi Arabia as part of Operation *Desert Shield*. This was

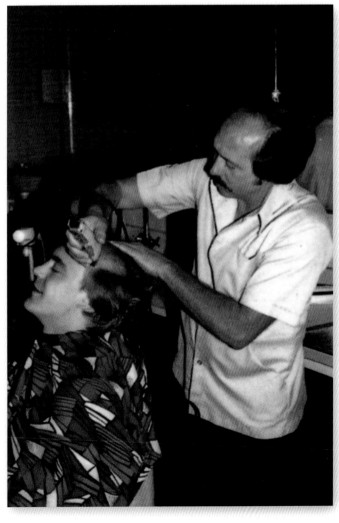

Welcome to the US Army. A recruit has his hair shorn; he had to pay for his "scalping." Once training had been completed they could let their hair grow out, to a point, but most kept it short, especially on the sides and back. In the desert they kept it very short because of the heat and for sanitary reasons.

followed by months of build-up and preparation for the actual liberation of Kuwait, a feat requiring only three days for Operation *Desert Storm* – The "100-hour war." There were 37 US infantry battalions deployed to Saudi Arabia. The ground war is often remembered for the sweeping maneuver of "heavy forces," armored battalions with their M1 Abrams tanks, armored cavalry squadrons mounted on their more modern steeds, M3 Bradley cavalry vehicles and M1 tanks, and mechanized infantry in their M2 Bradleys. Of the infantry battalions, 18 were airborne and air assault and 19 were mechanized infantry.

A **M2A1 BRADLEY INFANTRY FIGHTING VEHICLE**

Three versions of the M2 Bradley infantry fighting vehicle (IFV) were employed. The M2 (a.k.a. M2A0 or "vanilla Bradley") was introduced in 1981, the M2A1 in 1987 and the M2A2 in 1988. Including the M3 cavalry fighting vehicle (CFV) there were 2,200 Bradley fighting vehicles (M2 and M3 were collectively called BFVs) deployed to the Gulf. The Bradley was the squad's tactical transport, home, fire support, and an integral part of the unit that influenced its organization.

The Bradley underwent a lengthy and troubled development. The goal was to provide a well-armored combat vehicle able to keep pace with the M1 Abrams tank, and allow the squad to fight from it. Previous APCs were "battle taxis" in which the squad merely traveled as passengers. They were blind to the terrain and situation they would face when dismounting and could not fire on the enemy without exposing themselves.

The media were highly critical of the Bradley, faulting it for being too cramped and having too high a profile (it would have been more cramped with a lower profile). They also criticized it for being vulnerable to antiarmor weapons and too costly.

The Bradley was a well-armed, high-speed vehicle with a high degree of survivability offering capabilities never before available to infantrymen. It mounted a 25mm M242 Bushmaster chain gun **(1)** in the two-man turret along with a 7.62mm M240C coaxial machine gun **(2)** and an external two-tube TOW launcher **(3)**. Two sets of four-tube M257 smoke grenade dischargers **(4)** were mounted on the front of the turret with grenade storage boxes beside them. These fired British red phosphorus grenades a short distance to conceal the vehicle with a white smoke cloud if engaged by antiarmor fire, allowing it to change course or withdraw. They could not be fired near dismounted troops as the phosphorus inflicted casualties. The Integrated Sight Unit (ISU) **(5)** for all turret weapons is on the turret's left top. It had a three-man crew, the commander (BC) **(6)** wearing the armored crewman's uniform and DH-132A combat vehicle crewman helmet, the gunner, and the driver. The driver's hatch **(7)** demonstrates how it provided protection when partly opened. The squad's duffle bags are stowed on the sides **(8)**. The M2 and M2A1 had two 5.56mm M231 firing port weapons **(9)** on each side and the rear ramp with periscopes. The M2A2 and all M3-series CFVs had only the rear FPWs.

The on-board armament provided substantial firepower, so much so that often the infantry did not have to dismount to defeat the enemy. They had only to dismount after the enemy had been destroyed or fled, and then to search the area and provide security.

The stabilized 25mm chain gun could be fired accurately on the move and was provided with a thermal imaging sight, the ISU, which also aimed the other weapons, allowing engagements in the dark, fog, rain, dust, and smoke. The gun could be fired semi-automatically, 100 rpm or 200 rpm intended for helicopters. Targets were typically engaged with 4–6-round bursts to almost 2,000m. Two magazines allowed the ammunition type to be selected. The 75-round magazine was for armor-piercing discarding sabot-tracer (APDS-T) while the 225-round magazine held high-explosive incendiary-tracer (HEI-T). Another 600 rounds were stowed.

To kill tanks the twin TOW II (Tube-launched, Optically-tracked, Wire-command link guided missile) could defeat any tank to 3,000m, which required a 16-second flight; the Bradley had to halt to fire this. The gunner had to keep the sight crosshairs on the target during its flight. There was storage space aboard the Bradley for five of the 152mm missiles, plus two in the launch tubes. However, two of these spaces were required to store Dragon missiles.

The Bradley was a big vehicle having a higher profile than the M1 tank it accompanied. While often criticized, this height was necessary as the vehicle was designed to accommodate 80 percent of males, to include 6ft-tall soldiers, in moderate comfort. The necessary turret also increased its overall height. It was heavy too, with a combat weight of 49,000 lb (22,200kg) – over 24 tons, about 9 tons less than a World War II M4 Sherman, and with much better protection than the M4. As heavy as it was, the Bradley reached a speed of 41 mph (66km/h) – 38 mph (61 km/h) for the M2A2 – and was amphibious with preparation. The M2 and M2A1 had a 500 hp diesel and the M2A2 a 600 hp. It was difficult to throw a Bradley's track and its availability rate was extremely high; few ever broke down.

CHRONOLOGY

(Only the arrival of heavy US divisions are listed.)

1990

August 2	100,000 Iraqi troops invade Kuwait.
August 6	Saudi Arabia requests US military support.
August 7	First US troops arrive in Saudi Arabia commencing Operation *Desert Shield*.
August 28	Iraq "annexes" Kuwait.
September	24th Infantry Division deploys.
October	1st Cavalry Division deploys.
November	Second wave of US forces begins deploying from Germany: 1st and 3d Armored Divisions with brigades of the 2d Armored and 3d Infantry Divisions. Deployment completed in January.
November 29	UN orders Iraqi forces to withdraw from Kuwait by January 15, 1991.
December	1st Infantry Division deploys.

1991

January 17	Operation *Desert Storm* commences with cross-border attacks at 0238 hours local time.
January 22	Iraqis ignite Kuwaiti oil wells.
January 29	Battle of Khafji (Iraqi cross-border probe), lasting until February 1.
February 20	1st Cavalry Division conducts feint.
February 22	Final ultimatum given to Iraq.
February 24	Ground War begins when Coalition forces invade Kuwait and Iraq at 0400 hours local time. US Army troops are the first to cross the border.
February 26	Saddam orders his forces to withdraw from Kuwait.
February 27	US and Saudi forces enter Kuwait City.
February 28	A ceasefire is ordered at 0800 hours local time.
March 2	Iraqi forces attempting to escape Kuwait are destroyed by 24th Infantry Division.
March 17	First US troops return to the United States.
March 28	Most US POWs are released.
June 8	A victory parade takes place in Washington.

ENLISTMENT

The US Army attracted all types of men and women motivated by a wide variety of dynamics. Some joined for reasons of patriotism and the desire to begin a military career. Many joined up to learn a skill – not necessarily the case for an infantryman, but for the more technical MOS. Although the infantry is often considered a simple non-technical MOS, this is far from true. There are scores of skills necessary to operate and maintain the many weapons, target acquisition, observation, communication, and navigation systems, to say nothing of the tactical, battlefield survival, land navigation, and NBC defense skills. There were powerful incentives to join the infantry.

It was here that leadership skills, teamwork, and the ability to work with others were the most critical skills in the Army. It taught a great deal in terms of self-confidence, initiative, and motivation. It was also highly physically demanding, and challenged each soldier to push himself to the limit, to see just what his capabilities and limitations were.

It was true that the poorly educated and less skilled tended to end up in the infantry, including many at the lower end of the US social scale. A score of 70 on the General Technical (GT) test (a form of IQ test) was necessary for the infantry. For comparison, a GT score of 110 was required for Special Forces or officer training.

The foremost motivation for youths to join the Army was admittedly the education benefits. These benefits were substantial, offering them thousands of dollars for college tuition, book fees, and living expenses. Troops were even encouraged to take night classes while in the Army. Branch colleges were found on or adjacent to bases. Attendance and study often proved difficult for infantrymen though, owing to their irregular training schedules, with multiple days spent in the field and on night exercises.

One assumed disadvantage of undertaking military service prior to college was that a soldier would begin studying three or four years after his civilian peers. However, in the meantime he would have gained a great deal of experience in leadership and people skills, developed confidence, and matured. His experiences made college less of a challenge and the self-discipline learned often made for better students.

There was little in the way of active recruiting on the Army's part. Recruiters might be present at high school career days and job fairs. Occasional ads were seen in car, hunting, sports, and bodybuilding magazines and on television, accompanied by the almost 20-year-old recruiting slogan of

Uniform issue at the Quartermaster's. The experienced civilian employees simply looked at a recruit and accurately judged his size for any and all garments.

Military pay
Soldiers were paid twice a month by direct deposit into their personal account at the bank of their choice. Before income tax and social security deductions, the Base Pay for soldiers with less than two years' service (1990 scale) was:

$669.60	E-1 less than 4 months
$724.20	E-1 over 4 months
$811.80	E-2
$843.60	E-3
$895.50	E-4
$960.00	E-5

For comparison, a 2nd lieutenant with less than two years' service had a monthly basic pay of $1,387.20. The platoon sergeant with over eight years' service made $1,572.00. Soldiers authorized separate quarters were paid approximately $155–252 without dependents and $278–361 with dependents, depending on their pay grade. They were also authorized $6.67 Basic Allowance for Subsistence (rations) per day. When deployed to *Desert Shield/Storm* they were authorized Hostile Fire ("Combat") Pay at $110 per month for all grades. They were also authorized $8–16 per month Foreign Duty Pay depending on grade, and if married $60 Family Separation Allowance. Combat pay and other allowances were non-taxable.

"Be all you can be." Mail-outs were also made to high school seniors approaching graduation. Several hundred Army Recruiting Centers were found in malls and strip centers, even in moderately sized towns, manned by over 4,000 professionally trained recruiters.

Recruits were required to be at least 18 years of age and were not to have reached their 36th birthday. 17-year-olds could enlist with their parents' permission. A high school graduation certificate or having passed the General Educational Development Test were key prerequisites, although a small percentage of non-graduates was permitted if they obtained sufficiently high entry exam scores; they were expected to pass the GED once in the Army. It was found that about 80 percent of high school graduate enlistees completed their first three years of service while only 50 percent of non-graduates did. GED holders fell somewhere in between.

When a potential recruit visited a recruiter he was provided literature; the recruiter might visit him and his family at home. The recruit would be given the Armed Services Vocational Aptitude Battery (ASVAB – "as-vab") to determine enlistment eligibility, before the recruiter spent any significant amount of time and effort on an individual. It was scientifically developed to ensure all enlistees would have a reasonable probability of completing military job training and performing successfully. A component test was the Armed Forces Qualification Test (AFQT), a composite of verbal and math tests. This was the primary enlistment screening; a minimal score was 31 out of 99 for high school graduates and 50 out of 99 for GED holders.

There were also height and weight standards to be met, and recruiters would often take potential recruits to a local park for light fitness training to prepare them. Recruits could not have a criminal record. In-processing was conducted at one of 65 Military Entrance Processing Stations (MEPS), where all applicants for the whole of the Armed Forces were processed. This consisted of two days of processing, a comprehensive physical, drug testing, eye and hearing tests, weight and body fat measurement, security clearance interview, and a great deal of paperwork. If from out of town an enlistee would be quartered in a hotel. Finally, he was sworn in by an officer, not necessarily an Army one, with other enlistees.

Two enlistment contracts were signed (DD Form 4/1 Enlistment/ Reenlistment Document: Armed Forces of the United States). The first was for the Delayed Enlisted Program (DEP), which assigned an individual to the Inactive Reserves from when the contract was signed to when he departed for active duty. He was not paid, received no benefits, and was not assigned to a drilling Reserve unit; it was merely an administrative act. The second contract was for active duty enlistment. Any promises made by recruiters for enlistment bonuses or the type of training were invalid unless they were listed in an annex in this contract. What was listed in the DEP contract was meaningless for active duty. Bonuses were based on the duration of the enlistment and MOS. This might amount to $2,000–$4,000. There were other benefits: complete medical and dental care was provided, most weekends were off once training was completed and assigned to a troop unit, especially payday weekends, and 30 days' leave were granted each year.

Enlistments could be from three to six years, but a term of three or four was common. Regardless of the active duty enlistment period, an individual enlisted for an eight-year obligation. The balance after active duty was fulfilled in the Individual Ready Reserve (IRR). This was a paper assignment, making him eligible for call-up in a national emergency. He was not assigned to a drilling unit and in all probability would never again don a uniform. Upon "separation" from active duty he might opt to join an Active Reserve or National Guard unit and attend weekend drills, annual summer camp, and other training. At the end of his eight years' obligation he would then be "discharged" from the armed forces, or he could choose to reenlist.

The recruit might spend a week or several months awaiting a training date. On the assigned date the recruit reported to the MEPS for brief physical, documents and status reviews, and was again sworn in for active duty. Bringing with them only a change of clothes, toiletry articles, and a few dollars, a small group of infantry enlistees would board a bus or airliner for Columbus, GA.

TRAINING

Enlistees reported to the Reception Station at Ft Benning in west-central Georgia on the Alabama stateline – "Home of the Infantry" – and were attached to the 30th Adjutant General Battalion (Reception) for a few days. Here things moved at a fast pace for the somewhat bewildered enlistees. They did more paperwork, received burr haircuts, another physical, inoculations and briefings, and were issued uniforms. They learned how to make bunks, store their uniforms in lockers, and about barracks life in general.

Basic training phase
They were assembled into a training company and the 200 trainees met their Drill Sergeants (DS – the Army used this term and not "Drill Instructor," which was a Marine term) wearing "Smokey Bear" hats and starched and tailored BDUs. They eyed the trainees with obvious disapproval. Loaded aboard 18-wheel "cattle trucks" they sat on the troop seats with their overloaded duffle bags between their legs unable to see over the trailer's high sides. They found themselves delivered to the Harmony Church area with its sandy, gently rolling terrain covered by pine and oak. This was a remote training area seven miles east of the main Ft Benning cantonment area.

More DSs, addressed only as "Drill Sergeant," were waiting for them, and they were run off the trailers under a barrage of shouting. They were dropped for seemingly countless push-ups on the hand-blistering hot asphalt. The "Day 1 shock effect" served to let trainees know who was in change and what their station was. This only went on for a couple of hours, but seemed endless to the disoriented trainees. Harassment continued through the day and into the night as the trainees organized into a company. Although the DSs were not supposed to swear or use abusive language, they did, and warned trainees it would not be a good idea to complain.

A typical company designation was Company D, 2d Battalion, 2d Infantry Training Brigade (1st Brigade provided light infantry training at Sand Hill, called "Sand

"More PT Drill Sergeant!" Physical fitness training was a daily routine. Gray flannel sweatsuits, marked ARMY in black, were issued, as were similar t-shirts and shorts.

TA-50 orientation. Table of Allowance 50 specified the gear issued to individual soldiers and was a common name for "web gear." Here recruits are talked through the gear to identify the many different components and how to assemble the array of belts, straps, and pouches.

Hilton" by 2d Brigade trainees owing to the modern air-conditioned barracks). It consisted of four platoons of four squads with the platoons nicknamed "Warriors," "Rangers," "Bulldogs," and other such names. Two or three DSs oversaw a platoon. Trainees, sometimes those with high school Reserve Officer Training Corps (ROTC) experience, were designated squad leaders and platoon guides; the latter managed the platoon in the absence of the DSs.

Rather than carrying out Basic Combat Training and Advanced Individual Training in different units, as had happened in the past, infantry training combined both of these stages under the One Unit Station Training (OUST) program. They would live in the same barracks and have the same DSs throughout their 13 weeks. Sometimes, one or two weeks were added to OUST as training requirements were changed. The first six weeks constituted basic training, while the remaining seven weeks consisted of 11M mechanized infantryman training.

The first couple of days were hard and intense, and most enlistees would question their decision to join the Army. Every single thing they did was wrong or not fast enough, resulting in being dropped for 10 pushups – "Drop and beat your face, Hero!" They had not a waking minute to themselves. Every moment was structured. Meals were rushed and the yelling went on. Enlistees tended to feel harassed, confused, and homesick, and felt they were surviving day-to-day.

The barracks proved depressing. These were "temporary," wood-frame, World War II-era, two-story "barns." The condemned white-painted barracks with their light gray roofs and dark green doors were older than the enlistees' fathers. They had no air-conditioning and were musty; with fans running day and night, it was impossible to keep dust out. Two squads were housed on each floor with double bunks in two rows. Each man had a double-wide, gray steel, wall locker; foot lockers were a thing of the past. They were lectured on barracks security, keeping track of their uniforms and equipment, and keeping their lockers padlocked.

Each company area, which they were restricted to except when undertaking training, consisted of the four platoon barracks, a company headquarters with supply and arms room, mess hall, and a day room, which they seldom saw the inside of in the first weeks. Other than the barracks, these were all one-story buildings. Divisional and other Army insignia, painted on fiberboard, decorated the exterior barracks walls.

After about a week the men began to acclimatize, and they became accustomed to the daily grind. Harassment lessened noticeably. Most enlistees were 18 to 20 years old, but some were older, even in their early 30s, and they would have an especially tough time. The day began in a rush at 0530 hours as 40-odd men shaved and brushed their teeth while pulling on BDUs. A quick platoon formation followed, with a roll call. Breakfast was an equally rushed affair, and then came a company formation. After this, the enlistees seldom knew where they were going or what they would be doing. This was initially a major concern for many, but by the second week they had accepted this, and loaded themselves into cattle cars or buses, or marched off, without question.

Basic training focused on the most vital skills for all soldiers: courtesy and customs of the service (when and whom to salute), Code of Conduct and the Geneva Convention, the military justice system, first aid, hand-to-hand combat, bayonet drill, NBC defense training, individual tactical training and battlefield survival, and more. A great deal of time was spent on one of the most disliked subjects, dismounted drill and ceremonies – how to march and move in formation. Much of each day was spent on physical training, the Army Daily Dozen with stretching and fitness exercises, two-mile runs and forced marches, and more push-ups followed by "enthusiastic" shouts for, "More PT Drill Sergeant!" Every morning the men would march over the 8th Division Road bridge to the PT field on the other side of Highway 29. This was all in preparation for the Army Physical Fitness Test (AFPT), which needed to be taken for the record and in order to graduate from Basic training. The score was based on age. A 17–20-year-old was required to do 42 push-ups in two minutes, 52 sit-ups in two minutes, and a 2mi run in 15 minutes and 54 seconds. There were also obstacle and bayonet assault courses. All of this physical activity was not just for fitness and endurance, but also served to improve agility, coordination, and aggressiveness.

Two weeks were dedicated to the 5.56mm M16A2 rifle. Some young men had fired .22 rifles, deer rifles, or shotguns, but had had no exposure to a modern assault rifle. Most had never fired a weapon. Training began with disassembly and assembly, maintenance, operation, shooting fundamentals, range and safety procedures. Every time these weapons were drawn from the arms room it resulted in meticulous cleaning. They first learned to "zero" the rifle, to adjust sight alignment to the bore. Field firing was then conducted at 75, 175, and 300m ranges. The trainees took turns coaching one another, and after firing on countless ranges could work their way up from never having fired a weapon

Cleaning an M16A1 rifle – a daily chore, executed every time weapons were drawn for training. "Ammo cans" were used to carry cleaning patches, bore brushes, and oils and lubricants.

to Expert level. They were taught to fire from prone, kneeling, squatting, standing, and foxhole positions. Two practice sessions of qualification firing were conducted before they fired for "record." Targets were positioned from 50 to 300m hidden among trees and brush on irregular terrain. The olive drab targets were silhouettes of actual-size men from the waist up. They were "popped up" by a remote-controlled mechanical device and exposed only for a few seconds before being lowered. The shooter had to observe for movement to detect and engage his targets among vegetation before they disappeared. Forty rounds were fired from different positions including foxhole. A score of 23–29 ranked the firer as a Marksman, 30–35 as a Sharpshooter, and 36–40 as an Expert. A score of 22 and below was unqualified, a "Bolo." Bolos were given second and

Recruits wait their turn in the chow line. Usually three men were allowed through at a time.

Practicing the foxhole firing position on the M16A1 rifle range. The Drill Sergeant calls out hits on the target hit counter, linked to the targets by buried cables, and the standing recruit records the scores on the score card.

third chances to qualify and received additional coaching. If they were unable to qualify they were "recycled" to the next training cycle, sometimes more than once. They did not start at the beginning, but were assigned to a company ready for the marksmanship phase.

Soldiers were also recycled for inability to accomplish other tasks. This was usually due to the inability to meet PT standards. Typically 20–30 percent were either recycled or discharged because of "inability to adapt to military life." This might be due to failure to follow and obey orders, or to adapt to group living, the inability to handle stress, or to accomplish or complete tasks, etc. Often this was simply due to disliking being yelled at, not fitting in, different expectations of the military, or the fact that the enlistee simply could not hack it. Personal problems at home were also a contribution.

Mess halls were operated by contracted civilian cooks – "spoons" – and there was no love lost between them and the soldiers assigned as kitchen police (KP). A trainee would draw KP every two or three weeks. It usually began at

0330 hours and might go on as late as 2200 hours. The most dreaded job was "pots and pans man." He was responsible for endlessly scrubbing the many large pots, pans, and utensils. "Dish washers" operated the conveyor-like dishwasher for dinning ware and silverware. "Dining room orderlies" – DRO – cleaned the tables and floors after each meal and took care of many other chores. The most "desirable" job was the "outside man." He manned the loading dock behind the mess hall. His job entailed carrying garbage to the dumpster, cleaning garbage cans, hosing off the loading docks, and carrying in food deliveries. Being outside, he was removed from the direct pestering of the "KP pusher."

While restricted to the company area during Basic training, Saturdays were only a half-duty day with possibly PT, an inspection, and admin work. Sundays were off and little was seen of the DSs. Writing letters home was encouraged and mail call was essential to maintaining morale. Platoons were occasionally granted telephone privileges to call home. With scores of men lined up at the banks of phone booths, calls were limited to 5–10 minutes.

Infantry training phase

The Basic phase was completed faster than most expected, with the enlistees evaluated on the CTT, AFPT, and rifle qualification. There was a short graduation ceremony and then they got their first weekend pass into Columbus. This was the first time married men had seen their wives since reporting for duty – if they made it to Columbus. Monday morning saw the start of infantry training. Harassment was noticeably reduced; the men now wore camouflage helmet covers and generally had weekends off. They might be granted an off-post pass or at least they were free to partake of the entertainment and activities offered on-post. They retained the same DSs, but more of the instruction was provided by NCOs in specialized training committees.

Individual training had become strongly institutionalized by the early 1980s. Gone were the days of field manuals providing guidelines for experienced NCOs to use as the basis of training combined with their practical experiences. In the mid-1970s a new training system was introduced, the Individual Training Evaluation Program. An extensive series of manuals were fielded prescribing the critical individual skills each soldier needed to know to perform in his MOS. These Soldier's Manuals were provided for each MOS and skill level and designated Soldier's Training Publications. The most basic was STP 21-1-SMCT, the Soldier's Manual of Common Tasks, Skill Level 1. This 1½-in-thick, "pocket-size," 730-page manual contained about 100 tasks that every soldier in the Army regardless of MOS and rank had to be able to perform. There was also an STP 7-11BCHM14-SM-TG, Soldier's Manual and Trainer's Guide-MOSs 11B, 11C, 11H, and 11M Infantry. The tasks were specified by task, conditions, and standards. A sample task was "Camouflage yourself and your individual equipment." The conditions were that he be given LBE, weapon, Kevlar helmet with camouflage cover and band, camouflage sticks (or other materials that could be used to camouflage exposed skin), burlap, sandbags, or cloth strips. The soldier would be wearing BDUs. The standards were that he should camouflage all exposed skin areas and individual

ABOVE
The Grenade Assault Qualification Course required the soldier to engage different types of targets at varied ranges using different throwing positions. Inert practice grenades were used.

BELOW
Learning how to probe for landmines. Helmets were removed to provide unrestricted vision, to prevent them from inadvertently falling off, and to remove large metallic objects from the area (not a concern with the Kevlar helmet).

equipment to avoid visual detection. The task description would then go on to outline camouflage techniques, use of materials, and evaluation. The successful accomplishment of tasks was graded on a "Go/No Go" basis – a soldier either met the standard or he failed.

Many of the tasks were highly technical and demanding. There were, for example, 21 tasks involving NBC protection ranging from care and use of different protective masks, use of detection and protective items, decontamination techniques, to use of the latrine while wearing MOPP gear in a contaminated environment. Eight tasks involved the M16A2 rifle. There were many more infantry-specific tasks, covering the full spectrum of technical and tactical requirements.

Soldiers underwent an annual Common Skills Test (CST), demonstrating their skills with selected tasks and the MOS-specific Skill Qualification Test (SQT). As complete as the tasks were, there was a problem with the system. Instructors could only teach exactly what was in the book and no more. They were prevented from passing along hard-earned practical knowledge, and what soldiers were being taught was designed only to pass the CST and SQT. Still, conventional wisdom was that if a soldier was proficient at the many tasks, he would perform well in combat. Practical knowledge would come with field experience.

Physical fitness training and forced marches continued. They would have to pass the AFPT again at the end of training. Training became more technical. Radio and field telephone training along with radio procedures, such as the use of pro-words and the phonetic alphabet, were conducted. Land navigation, map reading, and use of the compass were included, with an introduction to mine warfare. Squad tactical training, patrolling, and military operations on urbanized terrain (MOUT) were practiced. Familiarity training was also given on the Bradley fighting vehicle to include mounting and dismounting tactically, orientation rides, swimming the Bradley across Victory Pond, weapons firing, operating the vehicle's NBC protective system, and so on. Much emphasis was placed on weapons familiarization, covering the 5.56mm M249 squad automatic weapon, 5.56mm M231 firing port weapon, 7.62mm M60 machine gun, 9mm M9 pistol, 40mm M203 grenade launcher, and M72A3 and M136 ("AT4") light antiarmor weapons. They also undertook the Grenade Assault Qualification Course.

B **CLEARING IRAQI ENTRENCHMENTS**
One of the most frequent tasks the dismount squad was called upon to do was the clearing of Iraqi trenches and fortifications. They had trained long and hard for this in mockup trenches and "shooting houses" constructed of sand-filled tires built by engineers. They typically undertook this task as fire teams, usually of four men. Teams moved through the trenches and bunkers in tight formations – "stacking" – a clearing concept borrowed from police SWAT teams. An M16A2-armed rifleman (or antiarmor specialist not needing his Dragon) is the pointman **(1)**. The rifle-armed fire team leader **(2)**, a sergeant, led by example, his team following his actions. The M203-armed grenadier **(3)** was basically another rifleman in such close-quarters. The HEDP round required 14–27m to arm. This prevented friendly causalities if a round was accidentally fired into the ground within a squad or if it struck nearby vegetation. The M249-armed SAW gunner **(4)** brings up the rear as the "tail-gunner," ready to support the team with a high volume of automatic fire. The second fire team followed at a short distance, with the squad leader ready to provide support. The Bradleys **(5)** covered the fortification, with their turret weapons prepared to lay down suppressive fire. There would be little hesitation over lobbing an M67 frag into a trench section or room at the slightest sign of resistance. The attitude was simply that the Iraqis started the war and they were there to do their duty, set things right, and go home in one piece. Any Iraqi who attempted to resist was doomed. A Soviet-made 57mm S-60 antiaircraft gun, also used against ground targets, lies abandoned above the position **(6)**, as does an aging Soviet gas mask **(7)**.

The tactical training was realistic, with night firing, close-quarters live-fire exercises, with the last two weeks on a field training exercise (FTX) with tactical exercises and patrols. The night live-fire infiltration course saw the trainees low-crawling across a simulated battlefield with barbed-wire obstacles and craters. They crawled toward M60 machine guns firing live tracer rounds overhead, and demolition charges exploding around them. The crack of live rounds, streams of tracers, spraying mud blasted from craters, and floodlights periodically switched on to simulate flares gave trainees a fleeting sense of what actual combat would be like.

More testing followed in the last days of training, and soldiers would be thinking about where they might be going. A few days before graduation they received their orders. They would travel in groups or individually to their assignments. They might be surprised at the range of destinations: Georgia, Kansas, Texas, Colorado, Louisiana, Kentucky, West Germany, and South Korea. They were only assigned to a division and did not know what their battalion would be until arrival. The day before graduation those soldiers whose families would be attending the ceremony were given a day pass to visit them off-post. The graduation ceremony in Class A uniforms included displays and demonstrations of equipment followed by a pass in review by the graduating companies accompanied by a band. There was disappointment expressed by some that their DSs did not always congratulate them or shake their hand. They graduated, were handed a diploma, and were on their way by plane or bus to their new assignments.

DAILY LIFE

Army posts were self-contained cities, whose layout varied drastically, as did the type of buildings, being a mix of old and new. The post HQ on Ft Hood, TX was a modern, sprawling, three-story building rivaling a corporate headquarters built in the 1980s, while the Ft Polk, LA HQ was a far-too-small, wooden building dating from 1941. The oldest dated from World War II, and comprised wood-frame "temporary" structures, which had been "modernized." Concrete or cinderblock buildings dated from the 1950s. In the late 1970s and 1980s posts were in need of renovation and upgrading to accommodate a volunteer force. A much larger percentage of soldiers were married and had children. Instead of two-year conscripts and three-year volunteers, the Army was manned by three, four, and six-year volunteers, with many more making a career of it. To attract and retain soldiers they needed better quarters and facilities. With increased pay, even PFCs might have automobiles, a luxury usually only possessed before by NCOs. Parking lots now surrounded quarters.

Gone were the days of open, squad-bay barracks. The new apartment-like barracks and modernized older barracks often offered two, two-man rooms adjoined by a common bathroom and shower. Built-in lockers or even closets and drawers were provided. This was the standard, but many barracks still had eight-man rooms, with partitions and double-wide wall-lockers, and a single "gang" type latrine and showers per floor. The few World War II-era wooden barracks still in use had a latrine and gang shower only on the ground floor. Virtually all barracks were air conditioned and centrally heated. The apartment-type barracks were administered by Post Housing rather than by the units. Troops could opt to live off-post, usually sharing an apartment or mobile home with one or two other soldiers. On-post family housing was available, or families could rent or buy an off-post home. Soldiers living off-post were granted quarters allowance and separate rations allowance. When they ate in dining facilities and consumed meals in the field, including MREs, during training, they paid.

Posts on which divisions were based were large, and on-post facilities and activities for soldiers and their families were plentiful: movie theaters, playhouses, chapels, bowling alleys, sportsmen's clubs (shooting and fishing), sports fields, swimming pools, automotive craft shops, carwashes, woodworking shops, gymnasiums and fitness centers, libraries, arts and craft shops; officer, NCO, and E1 through E4 clubs; commissaries (large grocery stores), shoppettes (convenience stores), Class 6 (liquor) stores, laundromats, barber shops, post exchanges (main, branches, mini malls), military clothing sales stores, clothing re-sale shops, post offices, banks, travel agencies, and fast food restaurants (including national chains) all featured. Prices were only slightly lower than on the outside, but there was no sales tax. There were also schools, daycare centers, and Boy and Girl Scout activities and clubs ranging from martial arts to skydiving for soldiers and families. There was also an off-post, lakeside recreation center with all forms of outdoor activities including boat rental and cabins. Spouses could find employment as Department of Defense civilians, with a military contractor on-post, or with local businesses. Family members received medical and dental care from the Army and even veterinary services for pets. Posts even had their own television and radio stations and newspapers.

Pre-Gulf War unit training in peacetime; Bradley squad members pose behind their vehicle with 25mm chain-gun rounds slung over their shoulders. The blue projectiles indicate they are practice rounds. This unit still has the old M1 steel helmets. (Kevin J. Arlow)

Rank has its privileges

Soldiers soon learned that it was important to understand the enlisted rank system. There was more to it than just privates and sergeants. Pay grades were identified E1 through E9 – private to sergeant major. Rather than using the formal rank title, it was common to simply refer to ranks by their pay grade, for example, "There are only three E6s in the platoon," or, "He just got promoted to E5." The lowest rank was private 1 (E1), the entry-level pay grade. Soldiers could enter the Army at slightly higher pay grades if they had taken ROTC without accepting a commission or had a community college or university degree. Usually within a year they were promoted to private 2 (E2), having completed their MOS training and served in a unit. The next up the line was private first class (E3) or "PFC" typically achieved within two years, sooner for exceptional soldiers. Specialist (E4) was achieved within three years. Within the squad specialists were SAW gunners, grenadiers, Bradley drivers and gunners. Prior to 1986 this rank was referred to as specialist 4 (SP4), but became simply specialist (SPC) with the elimination of the specialist 5 and 6 ranks. Corporal was also an E4, but this rank was seldom seen and not found in the infantry. Fire-team leaders were sergeants (E5), commonly referred to as "buck sergeants." Squad leaders and Bradley commanders were staff sergeants (E6). The platoon sergeant was a sergeant first class (E7) and often referred to by their official abbreviation – "SFC." First sergeant (E8) was both the rank and position for the senior NCO in the company. Master sergeants, also E8, were found in battalion and higher staff positions. The command sergeant major (E9) was the senior NCO in the battalion and was the battalion commander's advisor on enlisted affairs. The "CSM", as far as the enlisted men were concerned, was the most powerful individual in the battalion, even

A US Army rank chart.

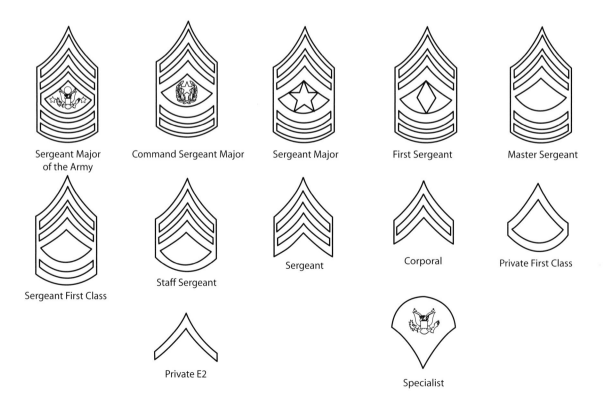

| Sergeant Major of the Army | Command Sergeant Major | Sergeant Major | First Sergeant | Master Sergeant |

Sergeant First Class

Staff Sergeant

Sergeant

Corporal

Private First Class

Private E2

Specialist

over the officers. A good CSM was involved in all aspects of the enlisted men's affairs and had a say in their promotion and assignments, who went to what schools, and who received recognition. Some CSMs were known for instigating and encouraging a high degree of "chicken shit," thriving on petty politics, meaningless harassment of the troops, and favoritism of cronies. This sometimes continued even in combat zones. Many other CSMs were excellent leaders, a positive influence on their troops supporting and encouraging them. Sergeant majors, also an E9, held staff positions at division level and higher. An E7 could be promoted directly to first sergeant and did not have to first hold master sergeant. The same applied to an E8 in either rank; he could be promoted directly to CSM and was not required to be a sergeant major first.

When addressing a soldier by rank, the system was simplified. Privates and PFCs were addressed simply as "Private." Specialists were "Specialist" and E5s, E6s, and E7s were addressed as "Sergeant." This used to apply to E8s as well, but in the 1980s they began to be referred to as "Master Sergeant" and "First Sergeant." E9s were "Sergeant Major" and "Command Sergeant Major."

How soldiers addressed one another within a platoon depended on unit practices. Some were more formal, referring to one another by rank and name, for example, "Private Gump" or "Sergeant Pepper." Others simply used last names, while others had a culture of nicknames, although senior NCOs were addressed more formally.

Enlisted men never addressed officers directly by the rank, but with "Sir." When naming an officer they used his rank and name, for example, "Where is Captain Cain?" Officer ranks too were often referred to by their pay grade: 2nd lieutenants – O1, 1st lieutenants – O2, captain – O3.

Some of the most realistic training conducted in the Army was at the National Training Center at Ft Irwin, CA. Each mechanized infantry battalion based in the States rotated through the intense brigade-level exercises approximately every 18 months. Here an infantryman guards a captured Opposing Forces (OPFOR) soldier.

THE MECHANIZED INFANTRY BATTALION

The mechanized infantry battalion was the soldier's extended family. It was a reasonably self-contained organization providing most of the combat support and service support it needed in battle. It received few attachments in combat beyond sometimes a combat engineer platoon and Stinger air defense missile teams, habitually one per company. Battalion strength was 47 officers and 775 enlisted men. The Bradley-equipped infantry battalion consisted of the headquarters and headquarters company, four rifle companies (A–D), and an antiarmor company (E). A battalion would be designated: 1st Battalion (Mechanized), 7th Infantry Regiment (1–7 IN (M)). Some battalions carried cavalry lineage and were designated, for example, 2–5 CAV (M). There was no actual regimental echelon; it was strictly a historical connection.

Desert Storm mechanized infantry battalions

Division or Brigade/Battalion	Bradley models
1st Cavalry Division (less elements)[1] 2–5 Cav	M2A2
1st Infantry Division (Mech) 2–16 Inf, 5–16 Inf, 1–41 Inf	M2
1st Armored Division 6–6 Inf, 7-6 Inf, 1–7 Inf, 4–7 Inf	M2A2
3d Armored Division 3–5 Cav, 5–5 Cav, 4–18 Inf, 5–18 Inf	M2A1
24th Infantry Division (Mech) 2–7 Inf, 3–7 Inf, 3–15 Inf	M2A1, some M2
1st Bde, 2d Armored Division 3–41 Inf	M2A2, some M2A1
197th Infantry Brigade (Mech) 1–18 Inf, 2–18 Inf	M113A3, some M113A2

Note

[1] 2d Brigade, 1st Cavalry Division was unique in that its battalions were permanently organized with a mix of mechanized and tank companies. 1–8 Cav and 1–32 Armor had one mechanized and three tank companies while 1–5 Cav had two of each and was rated as a mechanized battalion, while the other two were tank battalions.

Referred to as "HHC" or "Head and Head," the headquarters and headquarters company consisted of two mutually inclusive elements. The "Headquarters" consisted of the CO, XO, the four principal staff officers (S1 – personnel, S2 – intelligence, S3 – operations and training, S4 – supply), a couple of special staff officers, and the command sergeant major. The HQ company contained both combat support and service support elements. It had a small headquarters with the CO, XO, first sergeant, clerk, and a few other men. There was also a small battalion HQ section with staff NCOs and enlisted men who worked for the staff. The scout platoon's primary mission was reconnaissance and was not intended to conduct independent offensive, defensive, or retrograde operations like armored cavalry units. It could provide limited security and assist with battalion movement control. The platoon had six M3 cavalry fighting vehicles (CFV). The mortar platoon had six 4.2in M30 mortars mounted in M106A3 carriers. These were the battalion's only

STATESIDE MECHANIZED INFANTRYMAN

Whether stationed in the Continental United States (CONUS) or West Germany, the BDU was the standard field and daily duty uniform. Figure **1** wears the BDU field cap. Figure **2** wears the Kevlar helmet with luminescent "Ranger eyes" on the back of the "camo band." The All-Purpose Lightweight Load Bearing Equipment, commonly called "ALICE gear," included the equipment belt ("pistol belt"), "Y-strap suspenders," two small-arms ammunition cases ("ammo pouches") each holding three 30-round magazines, M9 bayonet, plastic entrenching tool carrier, 1qt plastic canteen with M1 NBC drinking cap (with nesting canteen cup), and first aid pouch on the suspender strap. A none-too-popular requirement was the way in which BDU jacket sleeves were to be rolled up; the jacket had to be removed to do this. (**3A**) The sleeve was pulled back on itself, then (**3B**) rolled up two turns. The excess end was then folded down over the roll (**3C**) concealing the reverse side of the fabric. (**4A**) The M9 multipurpose bayonet system (MPBS) had a 7.25in blade (12in overall) with a serrated back edge (the old M7 bayonet was also still in use). (**4B**) The plastic scabbard had a sharpening stone behind the carrying strap. The hole in the bayonet's blade was fitted to a lug on the scabbard tip as a wire-cutter. There was also a screwdriver blasé on the scabbard tip. (**5A**) The inside of the Kevlar helmet had a foam "donut" comfort pad. (**5B**) The helmet is also shown without the "camo cover," revealing its shape. (**6**) M17A1 protective mask without the hood. (**7**) A mask insert frame for prescription eyeglasses. (**8**) M58A1 training NBC decontamination kit. (**9**) Lensatic compass (carried in an additional first aid pouch). (**10**) Clear plastic 5 x 5in scale and protractor for determining coordinates on maps. (**11**) Three-way folding entrenching tool. (**12**) Canteen cup and canteen cup heating stand. (**13**) Fuel tablet carton containing three fuel packages, each with one "heat tab."

mortars. The communications platoon provided radio and field telephone support for the HQ and operated the message center. The largest platoon and among the most important was the support platoon. It was organized into an HQ and ammunition, fuel, transportation, and mess sections. It delivered rations, ammo, and POL (petroleum, oils, lubricants) to the companies. There were also small mess teams for attachment to each company. The medical platoon operated the battalion aid station, provided a medic to each rifle platoon, and had an evacuation section with M113A3 armored ambulances. The maintenance platoon maintained, recovered, and repaired unit vehicles. It consisted of an HQ and inspection and quality control, maintenance administrative, recovery support, and maintenance sections, plus company maintenance contact teams. There were two M2 Bradleys (CO and S3) and six each M113A3 APCs and M577 "High Hat" CP vehicles in the HHC used by staff sections, mortar fire-direction center, and mobile aid station.

The four rifle companies had an HQ equipped with an M2 Bradley for the CO, an M113A3 APC for the first sergeant, two HMMWVs, and two 2½-ton cargo trucks for rations, supplies and unit equipment along with a cargo trailer and a water trailer. The three rifle platoons had four Bradleys. Companies were typically referred to by their phonetic alphabet letters: Alpha, Bravo, Charlie, and Delta.

There were two internal platoon structures. Most units used the old organization of three rifle squads, one per Bradley. On paper these squads had a squad leader (SSG), two fire team leaders (SGT), two grenadiers (SPC), two SAW gunners (SPC), an antiarmor specialist (PFC), and a rifleman (PFC). In reality there was only room for six or seven men in a Bradley. The mortar forward observer (FO), his radio-telephone operator (RTO), and aidman rode in the platoon commander's No. 1 Bradley while the platoon sergeant commanded No. 4 track. A few men had to be split from their squad and ride in the No. 1 track. It was a moot point, as platoons were without exception understrength.

Hundreds of troops were housed in warehouses as they arrived in the Gulf, and waited for their equipment to arrive by sealift. There was noise for 24 hours a day, it was crowded, and it smelled worse than a locker room.

OPOSITE
A rifle squad, recently issued the 5.56mm M249 squad automatic weapon (SAW), undertakes orientation training on this. Two were supposed to be issued to squads, but mechanized infantry units mostly received only one during the Gulf War.

After days of waiting the unit's equipment finally arrived. Kit had to be signed for, inspected, and readied for overland travel and combat.

Some units organized under the new section concept with two squads, a better organization taking into account the limited seating capacity. The Bradleys operated with two per A and B Sections, A Section under the platoon leader (No. 1 track) and B under the platoon sergeant (No. 3 track) with 1st Squad split between the two A Section tracks and 2d Squad riding in the B Section Bradleys. The eight- or nine-man squads consisted of: squad leader, two fire-team leaders, two SAW gunners, two grenadiers, an antiarmor specialist, and a rifleman. The actual mix varied depending on weapon availability. The FO, his RTO, and aidman were split up between tracks.

The antiarmor company (Echo) had three platoons with four M901 improved TOW vehicles (ITV) plus four M113A3s. The platoons typically split into two sections and would be attached to rifle companies, but some ITVs might be held in reserve. Because of the difficulty experienced by ITVs in keeping pace with M2s and M1s, they were often all held back to reinforce engaged units. The ITV mounted an elevatable, two-tube missile launcher. The nine mechanized battalions deploying from Germany lacked antiarmor companies.

Battalions seldom fought "pure," that is, without cross-attachments. They typically attached one of their rifle companies to a tank battalion and in turn received a tank company. Along with other attachments the battalion became a "battalion task force" identified, for example, TF 2-16 Infantry. Likewise platoons might be cross-attached between companies, a tank platoon attached to a rifle company in exchange for a rifle platoon. This was a "company team." Not all companies in the TF were so organized – usually just one or two if any. In action the battalion commander might simply wait until an engagement occurred then temporarily order a tank platoon to reinforce a rifle company as necessary. The AFV's high-speed mobility, reliable communications, and open terrain permitted such maneuvers.

Armored divisions generally had four mechanized and six tank battalions while mechanized infantry divisions had five of each. There were exceptions in the mix and some divisions had only two brigades, their third brigade being a National Guard Round-out brigade, which did not deploy to the Gulf in late 1990.

WEAPONS

The infantry was provided with a selection of effective weapons, many of which had entered service in the last 10 years. However, whilst there were a few new weapons and improvements had been made to others, the 1990 infantryman was armed not much differently to an infantryman in Vietnam.

Some recruits had reservations about the 5.56mm M16A2 rifle, which carried a poor reputation from Vietnam. The problem was actually the early XM16E1 rifle, which was prone to jamming, especially if insufficiently cleaned. Many of these problems were corrected in the M16A1, but there were still issues. In 1985 a much-improved version was adopted, the M16A2. It was more rugged, possessed better ergonomics, and although it was semi-automatic it did possess a three-round burst capability. It was thought that by limiting the rate of fire to three-round bursts it would be more accurate and reduce the expenditure of ammunition in uncontrolled automatic fire. Other changes included a different rifling twist to allow it to use the new M855 Belgian-designed round with a heavier bullet. There were many refinements ranging from the design of the flash suppressor, new sights, increased barrel strength, stronger stock, and the redesigning of the forearm to allow it to be gripped by a smaller person. The M16A2 was light (8.76 lb – 3.99kg) and easily handled (36.63in – 1,066mm), and the light ammunition allowed the carriage of a significant basic load. Riflemen carried a minimum of seven 30-round magazines, for a total of 210 rounds. The troops were surprised when a drill sergeant told them that their rifle, which they simply called the "em-sixteen," cost almost $600.

Arriving in the desert. They may have been mechanized infantry, but they marched on foot to many of their training exercises, range firing, and so on.

The M203 grenade launcher was mounted under the forearm of the M16A2, adding 3 lb to its weight. The "two-oh-three," adopted at the end of the Vietnam War, provided the squad with a point and area fire weapon throwing high-explosive dual-purpose rounds as well as pyrotechnic signals.

The third key weapon in the squad's inventory was the M249 squad automatic weapon, the SAW. This was a Belgian-designed FN Minimi light machine gun firing the same 5.56mm round as the M16A2. It could be shoulder- or hip-fired and was provided with a bipod. For a weapon of its capabilities it was relatively light at 16½ lb (7.5kg). It was fed by a 200-round, disintegrating metallic-link belt. The belt was contained in a plastic detachable magazine. This was one of the weapon's main problem areas: the rounds rattled, the belt sometimes detached itself, and after expending part of the belt the remaining belt might become tangled inside after the weapon was jolted about. Overall it was considered reliable. The SAW also had a port in which an M16A2 magazine could be inserted. Most SAW gunners carried three magazines. The gun fired at 750–850 rpm, slightly faster with the 30-round magazine. While the SAW had been adopted in 1982, its initial issue was to the Ranger battalions, 82d Airborne Division, and light infantry units. By the time of the Gulf War many mechanized infantry were still waiting to receive it. A thousand were purchased from FN, but many squads received only one instead of the specified two.

Even though squads may have had only one or even no SAWs, each squad did have a 7.62mm M60 machine gun, known as the "Pig." Dating from 1959, the M60 was a tried and proven weapon. There was no dedicated crew and it would be a carried by a designated rifleman if needed, or a SAW gunner if this weapon was missing. It was a comparatively heavy weapon at 23.1 lb (10.5kg), but was fed by disintegrating metallic-link belt issued in 100-round containers, with an output of 550 rpm. It was provided with a quick-change barrel.

One of the most unusual small arms in the US inventory was the M231 firing port weapon. Adopted in 1979 it was similar to the M16A1 rifle. The internal recoil and buffer design were different and it only produced fully automatic fire, at 1,200 rpm. The FPW was designed to be fitted in swiveling firing ports on the Bradley, two in each side and two in the rear ramp of the M2 and M2A1. The M2A2 had only the two rear ramp guns, the other ports being sealed. This allowed squad members to engage close-range enemy troops and positions while mounted in the vehicle. It had no sight; its aim being corrected by the use of 100 percent tracers. It fired the older, lighter M196 tracer used in the M16A1. M16A2 ammunition was not supposed to be used in the FPW, but could be if necessary. In an emergency the FPW

D **INFANTRY TRAINING WITH THE 40MM M203 GRENADE LAUNCHER**
The two 40mm M203 grenade launchers assigned to a rifle squad were considered to provide one-third of the squad's firepower. Most soldiers were familiar with the "two-oh-three" from movies, but were disappointed to learn that, rather than producing a billowing fireball that flipped automobiles, it only created a small cloud of gray smoke and dust. The M433 high-explosive dual-purpose (HEDP) provides a 5m fragmentation casualty radius, but will penetrate up to 2in of armor, 12in of wood, 16in of sand-filled cinderblock (two layers), and 20in of sandbags (two layers). A grenadier could fire 6–7 rpm at up to 350m for area targets and 150m for point targets. It is also provided a variety of colored smoke and flare rounds for signaling and marking. The M781 practice round was used for training and generated a puff of yellow or orange smoke. Rather than the expensive Kevlar "Fritz helmet," trainees used the old M1 steel helmet. They donned a camouflage cover when entering the infantry training phase of OSUT. Trainees acting as coaches donned conspicuously marked helmets. The safety paddle signals the control tower that the grenadier is ready to fire. The reverse side is red, and is used to signal ceasing fire.

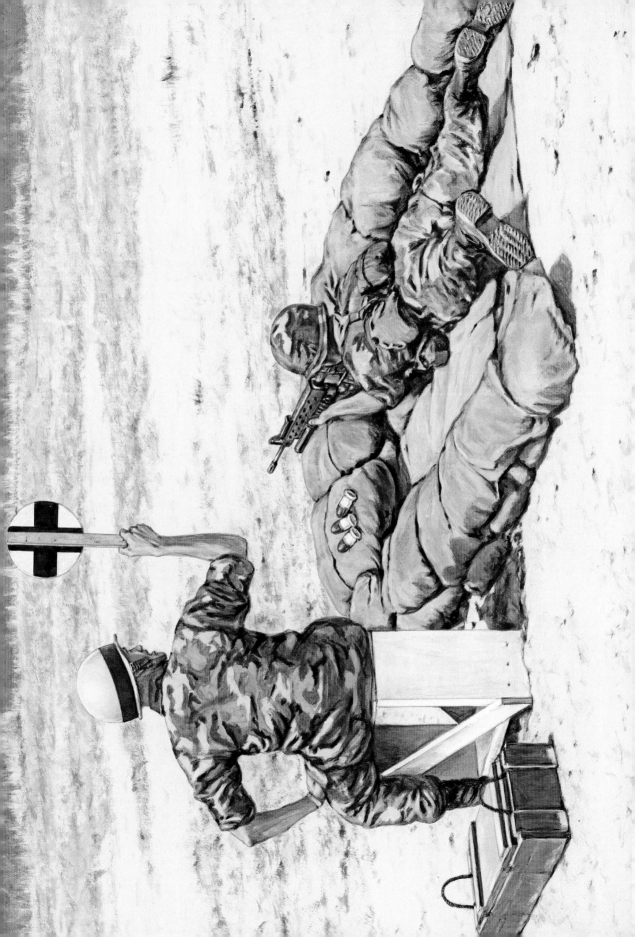

could be fired handheld, but this was discouraged owing to its high rate of fire, difficult to control muzzle climb, and overheating of the mounting ring, which could burn the hand; ear protectors also had to be worn.

Each squad had an M47 Dragon antitank wire-guided missile (ATGM). Adopted in 1973, the Dragon II warhead was introduced in 1985, featuring improved penetration. It had a 1,000m range and the 140mm warhead could, under ideal conditions, penetrate 18in of armor. It was heavy though, with the missile weighing 23.6 lb (10.7kg) and the tracking unit 15.2 lb (6.9kg). It was designed primarily as an antiarmor weapon and was of only limited use against other targets. When fired the missile had to be guided to the target via control wires by the gunner, who kept the launch unit's sight centered on the target. It required an 11-second flight at maximum range. Little use was made of these weapons during the Ground War, it being considered a "last resort."

Two weapons were issued on an as-needed basis. The M67 fragmentation grenade, simply known as the "frag" or "baseball grenade," dated from Vietnam. Looking like a slightly squashed tennis ball, it took the form of a smooth steel sphere with a pre-fragmented liner.

Squads typically carried three M136 light antiarmor weapons. While designated an LAW like the M72-series LAW it replaced, it was more commonly called the "AT4," its Swedish designation. This was an 84mm, rocket-like weapon firing a high-explosive antitank (HEAT) warhead that could penetrate up to 400mm of armor at a range of up to 200m. The AT4 was none too effective against bunkers. The HEAT round could penetrate sandbags and sand-filled crates, but unless enemy were in line with the jet-like penetrating blast others in the bunker might only be wounded by secondary fragmentation and there was little blast over-pressure. It was issued as a round of ammunition. Its 40in launch tube served as its shipping tube and weighed 14.8 lb (6.7kg).

APPEARANCE

Uniforms

The 1990 infantryman's appearance had changed little since the early Cold War era. In their first days in the Army trainees were issued a complete set of uniforms. There were three basic uniforms, and the number of components had been trimmed down by the adoption of multipurpose clothing items.

One set of uniform, the Army Green uniform, could be worn in two configurations. The Class A uniform consisted of a dark green coat and trousers. The open collar coat displayed pleated breast pockets and concealed skirt pockets, all pockets with flaps. The pockets and front opening were secured by gold-colored buttons. The fabric was a mid-weight polyester blend suitable for all seasons. A pale gray-green shirt, incorrectly called "mint green," completed the uniform. A black necktie and black web trousers belt with a gold-colored solid rectangular buckle accompanied it. Many soldiers purchased buckles and replaced the belt tip with pieces that required no polishing. Rather than issue web belt, a more comfortable elasticized version was often purchased. Only the garrison cap was issued. The unit crest (see below) was worn on the left side 1in from the front. The round-visored service cap, also known as the "bus driver" or "flying saucer cap," was optional purchase and only required by officers. Highly polished, low-quarter dress shoes were worn with black socks. Some soldiers purchased patent leather shoes to avoid the chore of spit-shining. Soldiers gave "Greens" mixed reviews. While many liked this uniform, many others felt it did not offer a military enough appearance, looking too much like a business suit, and disapproved of the color, especially the "mint green" shirt.

Tracked vehicles were hauled to desert assembly areas aboard heavy equipment transporters. This not only saved time, but more importantly preserved tracks, road wheels, engines, and transmissions for future combat.

M2 Bradley infantry fighting vehicles were typically festooned with all manner of gear: duffle bags, ammunition boxes, oil and lubricant cans, ration boxes, spare road wheels, and usually at least one roll of concertina wire (approximately 50ft in length when stretched out).

Embroidered gold-yellow on Army Green, rank insignia were worn centered on the upper sleeves. The "unit patch" – shoulder sleeve insignia – was on the upper left shoulder a half-inch below the shoulder seam. The rare Vietnam combat veteran among NCOs wore his former unit patch on the right shoulder – a "combat patch." The "unit crest" (distinctive unit insignia) – a small enameled badge – was worn centered on the coat's shoulder straps. Branch of service insignia, a gold-colored disc with crossed rifles was pinned to the left collar with the U.S. disc on the right. Infantrymen wore robin's-egg blue plastic backings with the discs. They also wore the infantry shoulder cord on the right shoulder. The infantry was the only branch authorized these distinctions. Individual award ribbons were worn over the left breast pocket and special skill badges either above the ribbons or on the pocket flap, depending on the type. Marksmanship badges were also worn on the pocket flap. Unit award ribbons, in a gold-colored frame, were worn above the right pocket. Depending on the regiment these unit awards represented unit distinctions in World War II, Korea, and Vietnam. While not in the unit when the award was granted, soldiers wore them as long as they were assigned to the unit. Above the framed ribbons was a third unit crest. For first-hitch soldiers this was usually the same as their current unit. For longer serving troops it was often the regiment they had first served in, their "parent" regiment. It was a rather artificial system, for the unit really was not a true parent one for the soldier in that he might never again serve in that regiment, even if he turned out to be a 20-year "lifer." The system was incompletely developed as the Army personnel system did not support the concept. Soldiers were assigned only where they were needed, without regard to any "parent regiment." On the right pocket flap a black plastic tag with the soldier's last name was engraved in white. On the left lower sleeve diagonal service stripes – "hash marks" – were worn, each representing three years' service.

The Class B uniform was an abbreviated Class A with the same Army Green trousers and gray-green shirt, but without the coat. In the summer a short-sleeve shirt was worn without the necktie. If the coat was worn with the short-sleeve shirt the tie was added, but it could be removed with the coat.

In the winter a long-sleeve shirt was in order and the necktie was required even without the coat. Insignia and decorations were as per with the coat, with some exceptions. Shoulder patches were not worn, nor were any other insignia required to be sewn on. Sergeants and higher displayed their rank in the form of black, slip-on shoulder strap marks with small gold-colored embroidered chevrons and a narrow gold-colored stripe across the bottom. E4s and below displayed gold-colored, pin-on rank insignia on their shirt collars. Unit crests were not worn on the shoulder straps. Soldiers had the option not to wear ribbons on the Class B shirt, although they usually wore miniature special skill badges. Nor did they wear decorations on the shirt when the coat was worn. Besides wide dislike for the shirt's color, it too presented a poor military image, and the fabric was too light giving a rumpled appearance. Holes made by decoration pins permanently damaged the fabric. A heavier fabric version with more military-appearing pleated pockets was available, but many still had the older shirts.

A black London Fog overcoat, doubling as a raincoat, included a zip-in liner for cold weather. Black leather dress gloves were provided. Optional purchase cold weather items were available in the form of a black, pullover, British-style "wooly-pully" sweater and a black, waist-length windbreaker. The only insignia worn on these black garments was the slip-on shoulder strap rank insignia, although the plastic nametag and parent unit crest were worn on a square black patch on the sweater.

A more popular uniform and the one soldiers spent the most time in was the battledress uniform (BDU). Loosely based on the Vietnam-era jungle fatigues, BDUs were printed with a four-color, woodland camouflage pattern. The shirt, officially called a jacket, had yellow patch pockets on the chest and skirt. All insignia sewn on the jacket were embroidered black on olive green. Even unit shoulder patches were subdued. A "U.S. ARMY" tape was sewn over the left pocket and a nametape over the right. Black sew-on or pin-on rank insignia were worn on the collars. The trousers were loose-fitting with internal front and hip pockets plus pillow cargo pockets on the thighs. Their cuff-ties allowed them to be tied off without having to blouse them into boots. There were still complaints about the BDUs, as with any uniform. The design of the jacket pockets made them virtually inaccessible when web

Many Bradleys were fitted with add-on armor. The driver's and engine compartment hatches are open. The box-like twin TOW antiarmor missile launcher is folded in the travel position on the left side of the turret.

Bradley IFVs lined up in the assembly area. It was common practice to fly small American or state flags on radio antennas – a Texas flag flutters on the center Bradley. Army regulations prohibited the display of state flags unless all were simultaneously displayed, but unit officers usually turned a blind eye.

gear was worn. The knees, seat, and elbows had reinforcing patches, which, while practical, made the uniform hotter. BDUs were considered too hot for summer and tropical use and a lightweight rip-stop version began to be issued in 1986. Regulations did not limit the wear of "heavyweight" and "lightweight" BDUs to particular seasons; they were worn at the soldier's discretion, but light and heavy components were not to be mixed. The BDU warm weather cap was based on the old "patrol cap" or "ranger cap" from the 1950s. Pin-on rank was worn on the front.

Accompanying the BDU was a heavy field jacket of water-repellent cloth bearing the same woodland pattern and insignia as the BDU shirt. The jacket by itself was not all that warm, comprising just three layers of fabric, but a removable battened liner was available. Underwear included a light brown undershirt and boxer shorts plus olive green cushion-sole boot socks. Olive green underwear had been used, but was replaced by a more universal brown with the introduction of the desert BDUs or desert camo uniforms (DCU).

Desert apparel

With increasing involvement in the Middle East, including peacekeeping operations in the Sinai and exercises with Egypt, the desert battledress uniform (DBDU) was introduced in 1982. This featured a six-color pattern based on the rocky, gravely deserts of the southwest US. Because of the gravel effect they were called "chocolate chips." The problem with this pattern was that it was inappropriate for the largely sand deserts of the Middle East. A new three-color sand pattern was introduced during the Gulf War, but by the time the fighting was over very few had been delivered. Black-on-olive-green subdued insignia, as worn on the BDUs, were used on the DBDUs. It was not long, though, before Saudi manufacturers began turning out dark-brown-on-sand subdued insignia, but these were seen more in higher HQs and support units. A full-brim desert hat was issued with the DBDUs.

There were only enough DBDUs in war reserve stocks to clothe a single corps with two sets. With just two sets of DBDUs, Tuesdays and Thursdays became "green" days to wear woodland BDUs whilst DBDUs were laundered. In September it was ordered that all deployed troops would be issued four sets, but by the time production caught up the war was over. Troops from Germany deployed with woodland BDUs. The Iraqi commanders told their men that the troops from Germany were superior to those troops that had deployed earlier from the States, because they had been trained to fight Soviet forces; the truth was that both types had been trained for this role.

A lack of laundry facilities and necessity led to relaxed uniform standards in the desert. It was not uncommon to see woodland field jackets worn with DBDUs, mixes of "green" and "desert" insignia, and incomplete insignia, woodlands body armor, etc.

Sunglasses were the order of the day, something normally frowned on. Issue black leather boots were hot. Many wore olive drab or black canvas-topped jungle boots in the belief that they were "cooler," but the drainage eyelets let in sand and the sole's steel shank conducted heat. Some were able to purchase Saudi tan suede leather desert boots. With the winter rains just before the Ground War woodland pattern field jackets, olive green rain jackets, woodland Gortex cold weather suits, and sweaters appeared.

Individual equipment
Collectively, desert and cold weather clothing, bedding, and other individual equipment were called "Snivel Gear." In terms of load-bearing or carrying equipment, the All-purpose Lightweight Individual Carrying Equipment – known as ALICE, or simply LBE or LCE – was a bewildering array of belts, straps, pouches, and odd items. Made of olive green nylon, the gear was durable and reasonably well designed, taking into account lessons from Vietnam. It consisted of a "pistol belt" with a plastic clip buckle, Y-shaped suspenders, two "ammo pouches" each holding three 30-round magazines and pockets on the sides for two frag grenades, a first aid pouch with two field dressings (for entry and exit wounds or multiple fragment wounds) fastened either to the belt or to the suspenders at the shoulder opposite the shooting arm, and one or two 1-quart canteens. The olive drab plastic canteens were carried in nylon carriers with a small pocket for Halazone water purification tablets, and were fitted with M1 black plastic caps with a fitting for a protective

Meetings of leaders were constantly held at all echelons to coordinate training and daily activities, receive orders, and exchange information.

Clowning it up in the assembly area. Three of these soldiers wear olive green rain jackets. In the background are Abrams M1 tanks.

mask drinking tube. An M8 multi-purpose bayonet in a self-sharpening sheath was carried on the left side. Coupled to the sheath it could be used as a wire-cutter. Sand-colored gear was ordered, but very little was used in the war. Some troops were additionally issued 2-quart canteens carried by a shoulder strap. Mechanized infantrymen seldom carried entrenching tools. As most of their gear was left in the Bradley, they had no need for a rucksack, but most carried a "butt pack," officially a combat field pack. This was a small pack attached to the rear of the belt to hold an MRE, gloves, field cap, sun cream, chap stick, spare socks, and other personal items. Personal clothing and sleeping gear were carried in olive drab duffle bags secured to the outside of the Bradley. All this gear was called "battle-rattle."

Soldier protection was upgraded with the adoption of the Personal Armor System for Ground Troops (PASGT). The PASGT helmet was a major departure from the previous M1 steel helmet with its liner. It was made of ½in thick Kevlar, resulting in its being simply called a "kevlar" as well as a "bone dome" or "Fritz helmet" owing to its similarity to the German World War II helmet. It provided a higher degree of protection from ballistics and by means of the greater percentage of the head covered. While a cloth "camo cover" was provided, it was non-reversible. Separate woodland and "chocolate chip" covers were issued. As the desert pattern cover was not always available some units simply sprayed the olive green helmets a sand color. Others made crude covers from sand-colored burlap or woven plastic sandbag material. Sometimes a piece of desert-pattern plastic camouflage net was fastened over the helmet. Sew-on or pin-on rank insignia were usually fastened to the camo covers. An olive green elastic camouflage band was worn. Often "cat's eye" or "ranger eye" fluorescent tabs were sewn on the back of the band so that a man following in the dark could maintain contact. Many infantrymen marked their last name on the front of the camo band.

A desert assembly area demonstrates how tents and facilities were irregularly dispersed as a means of protection from artillery and missile fire and air attack. The two tractor-trailers in the center are refrigerated and contain fresh food. As crude as the base camps were, internal asphalt roads were laid in an effort to reduce dust.

The second component of the PASGT was the "body armor, fragmentation protection vest, ground troops." The troops called it "body armor", a "flak vest," or "PASGT vest." It consisted of 13 layers of Kevlar fabric with a high protecting collar, two pockets, and two grenade hangers. The outer cover was woodland pattern camouflage, but later slip-on desert camo covers were provided. While the vest could reduce fragmentation casualties by 20–50 percent, troops complained about its weight (7½–11 lb/3.2–4.9kg; it was issued in five sizes), heat, reduced ventilation, and restricted movement. The same complaints were leveled at the 3.1–4.2 lb/1.4–1.9kg helmet, which was also issued in five sizes. Regardless of its weight, after a few days of wear it became virtually unnoticed. Most troops inserted a foam comfort pad or "donut" in the helmet's crown.

BELIEF AND BELONGING

Few soldiers in 1990 expected to find themselves in a major Middle East war, or any war for that matter. Other than the relatively small-scale Panama intervention a few months previously and the even smaller 1983 Grenada expedition, the Army had not seen combat since 1972. The Iron Curtain was crumbling and it was already apparent the Soviet Union as such was living on borrowed time and was no longer a viable threat.

Cooks turn out pancakes on the grill inside a mobile kitchen trailer (MKT). The margarine and syrup came in No. 10 cans. Other breakfast foods, including scrambled eggs and omelets, were provided in tray-pack rations (T-rats).

The Army had been primarily oriented toward defending Western Europe from the USSR and Warsaw Pact. The only other significant threat was North Korea. Contingency operations in the Caribbean, Latin America, Africa, and elsewhere were considerations, but these were minor compared with a multi-division war.

Unit cohesion is an extremely important aspect affecting unit efficiency, capabilities, and morale. Turnover of personnel was an ongoing distraction, but this ceased with the beginning of the Gulf War. The Stop-Loss policy was initiated allowing involuntary extension past one's Expiration of Term of Service (ETS) from active duty, retirement, or separation. This of course disrupted individuals' post-Army plans and was of course unpopular, but it was essential to units that were rapidly deploying to combat. While made controversial by politicians opposing different conflicts, Federal courts have consistently found that service members contractually agreed that their term of service may be involuntarily extended. To release trained and experienced leaders, soldiers, and specialists from already understrength units would have been debilitating and few replacements were available.

Black and white "Bedouin tents" were purchased locally because there simply were not enough tents in the Army's inventory to meet the needs in Saudi Arabia and elsewhere around the world. In the foreground is a pair of urinal tubes.

Before deploying, many units were brought up to strength with men drawn from others. Regardless of all the confusion and turmoil of deployment, a benefit emerged. Unit assignments were stabilized. Out in desert base camps they had the unprecedented opportunity to train with all personnel present and not siphoned off for external battalion work details, schools, leave, and other training distractions. They were able to focus on training and develop their tactical and technical skills to a high degree. Teamwork at all echelons was finely honed. This was extremely beneficial for the coming events and was a great morale enhancer.

Regardless of the difficult conditions, heat, dust, sandstorms and other discomforts, hard work, repetitious training, and a questionable future, soldiers appreciated the opportunity to improve their proficiency and teamwork, and thus their chances of survival. They learned one another's strengths and weaknesses and those of their leaders too.

There is no such thing as a bad unit, only bad leaders. The Army has developed excellent leadership training programs for officers and NCOs. New soldiers soon learned that there were exceptional, good, and poor leaders and that lieutenants and sergeants could not be collectively stereotyped.

The majority of 2nd lieutenant platoon leaders received their reserve commissions from ROTC, which was undertaken during four years of college. The second source was the 14-week Officer's Candidate School (OCS) at Ft Benning. Small numbers of officers came from four years of training, resulting in an engineering degree, at the US Military Academy at West Point, NY. Regardless of their source of commission, infantry officers would soon undertake the 16-week Infantry Officer Basic Course (IOBC) where they learned the tactical and technical skills of an infantry leader. Over 70 percent of this training is in the field. Lieutenants assigned to mechanized units undertook the seven-week Bradley Leader Course, also attended by NCOs. Additionally, several NCOs in each platoon would attend the 12-week Bradley Master Gunner Course. Many officers would attend the nine-week Ranger

One of the less savory work details, burning out latrine drums after mixing in fuel. Fortunately the burning fuel mostly masked any other odors.

"Beach" volleyball was a popular pastime, with the terrain being ideal for it. The courts are marked off with "engineer tape" – 2in-wide white cloth ribbon tape used to mark minefield passage lanes and obstructions.

Course, essentially a leadership course rather than a "commando school." It was conducted at various sites in Georgia and Florida, and from 1983 included a desert phase that was first conducted in Texas and later Utah.

NCOs underwent a series of NCO development courses under the NCO Education System, beginning with the four-week Primary Leadership Development Course (PLDC) when specialists. Next was the 10-week Basic NCO Course (BNCOC – "B-knock") for sergeants and staff sergeants. The Advanced NCO Course (ANCOC – "A-knock") was for SFCs. There was also a nine-month Sergeant Major Academy, and specialist courses for NCOs such as Battle Staff NCO, First Sergeant's, and Master Fitness Trainer Courses.

Laundry day in the desert. Plastic washtubs were occasionally used to hand-wash clothing. If there was any breeze at all the clothes would end up covered in dust before they had time to dry.

Chow is served beside an M557 "High Hat" command post vehicle and an HMMWV. The soldiers are attempting to use the vehicle to shield them from driving rain. All wear rain jackets.

The Army had implemented an experimental COHORT Program (Cohesion, Operational Readiness and Training) in 1980. Unit cohesion is based on mutual trust, common experiences, and the spirit of self-sacrifice. The COHORT concept was to form companies and battalions from the ground up with recruits who underwent OSUT together and then retained the same NCO and officer leaders for three years. The units would first serve in the States then be assigned an overseas tour. Particularly high-quality soldiers were selected for these units and often were brighter than some of the NCOs. There were advantages, but the system failed owing to a serious lack of cooperation by the Army Personnel Command. It also forced leaders to remain in a position for three years while in other units a lieutenant might be rotated through rifle platoon leader, support or mortar platoon leader, and company XO slots, thus gaining much more experience when reassigned to another unit and promoted to captain. There was also resentfulness from non-COHORT units over their preferential treatment; the program was terminated in 1995.

Overall, while the average soldier did not care to be in the "sandbox," most made the best of it and possessed an overwhelming desire to train to a high standard, defeat the Iraqis, get the job done, and go home to loved ones.

They initially had a grudging respect for the Iraqi soldier and expected him to be a tough opponent. This was based on their performance in the 1980–88 Iran–Iraq War in which they had fought viciously and demonstrated a high degree of capability, especially in the defense. Iran had suffered 250,000–500,000 casualties. As the Air War, commencing on January 16, 1991, rolled on, and in the light of the dearth of offensive operations by the Iraqis and the number of defectors who gave up, this perception gradually changed. It was not long before the jokes circulated: "For sale, Iraqi rifles. Only dropped once." "A modification work order was directed for all Iraqi tanks. Backup lights were installed." "Did you hear about the new store chain in Iraq? Target." "What do Hiroshima and Baghdad have in common? Nothing… yet." The constant barrage of hollow propaganda from Iraqi spokesmen quickly became the butt of jokes. Baghdad Radio claimed that tens of thousands of Americans would die and that they were an army trained only in defensive combat. "Baghdad Betty" entertained the troops with her own propaganda. Regardless, there were still concerns that there might be a tough fight ahead of them. While the Iraqis were gradually crumbling, there was always the possibility that some units would show more fight, especially the much-touted Republican Guard.

LIFE ON CAMPAIGN

Deployment

The individual soldier's experiences in his deployment to the "sandbox" were as varied as his experiences in battle. A unit's notification of deployment was typically brief, and the ensuing rush to ready the unit was riven with "hurry up and wait" confusion, conflicting orders, delays, and schedule changes. Some units were alerted far enough in advance that they practice-fired every weapon from pistols to artillery and repainted their vehicles sand color. Tanks received new treads if less than 300 useful miles remained and artillery pieces with less than a 150-round service life received new barrels.

Vehicles and unit equipment had to be readied for shipment and packed in MILVAN and CONEX shipping containers. The vehicles were driven to seaports and underwent further preparation for loading aboard contracted ships.

Back at home station the troops continued to prepare. There was a great deal of administration – power of attorney granted to wives, Serviceman Group Life Insurance (SGLI) beneficiaries updated (typically $100,000), pay allotments, personal property placed in storage, and countless other necessities. They received so many inoculations they felt like pincushions: hepatitis A and B, polio, tetanus-diphtheria, typhoid, chicken pox, measles, yellow fever, and plague – just what kind of place was the Army sending them to? There was also a tuberculosis test and the inoculations of the controversial anthrax series; it was feared the Iraqis would employ biological weapons. Desert uniforms and equipment were issued with body armor, MOPP suits, and other chemical defense gear. Clothing and equipment were packed in two duffle bags, the A and B-bags, according to ever-changing packing lists. The A-bag held clothing, toilet kit, and whatever would be needed daily. The B-bag was for spare clothing and less needed items.

Serving chow from insulated M1944 Mermite 5-gal containers brought to outposts from the unit kitchen. The three aluminum "inserts" each held 11½ pints. Troops behind the server are picking up snacks and fresh fruit.

Christmas in the desert. The "tree" was fabricated using a woodland pattern camouflage net and simple handmade decorations. Relatives also sent decorations for the unit tree.

Typically, a battalion, after delays and false starts and being crowded into gymnasiums, would be bused to an Air Force base. They would fly by chartered airliner, typically with a stopover at JFK Airport in New York, Bangor in Maine, or Gander in Newfoundland, then on to Germany for a layover at Frankfurt or Rhein-Main. There they were housed in massive heated *Oktoberfest* tents with banks of trailers containing latrines and showers. Most military transports, C-141s and C-5s, were reserved for hauling critical supplies. There might be more delays, with long waits in warehouses or tent cities; then came the long flight into the Kingdom of Saudi Arabia escorted by F-16 fighters. Landing at Dhahran Airport on Saudi Arabia's Persian Gulf coast they were bused to the Port of Damman. There they lived in warehouses, with thousands of troops passing through. Chow lines were long for cold hamburgers and cold showers too.

Battalions traveled in multiple lifts, and after arriving it might be days or weeks before all elements assembled. Then there were long boring waits for their vehicles and heavy equipment to arrive by two-week sealift, interrupted by Scud warning sirens. Regardless of the apprehension of going into combat, with the stress and rugged conditions most troops were ready to get going. Anything was better than sitting and waiting.

In the meantime the troops were far from idle. There were countless work details, perimeter guard duties, weapons and equipment maintenance, morning PT and runs with and without equipment – acclimatization in the hot, dry environment being essential – and countless classes. Their protective masks and MOPP suits never left their sides, even in rear areas. Some training was conducted "MOPPed up," wearing the protective gear. Classes included chemical and biological protection, first aid, battlefield survival, land navigation, communications, weapons, and vehicle identification.

A major milestone was the day, or rather days, when vehicles and equipment arrived by ship. Drivers and support personnel were trucked to the seaport to receive the vehicles. This was no simple matter. The preparations for ship transport had to be undone. The vehicles were inspected for damage and proper operation, were prepared for normal operations, on-board equipment was re-stowed, and they were fueled. In the following days the vehicles were prepared, their oil was changed, and they were thoroughly inspected. They would be used in rough tactical training, often undertaking lengthy road marches to reach the unit's position, and then it would all be done again in preparation for the ground war.

Life in the desert

The day finally came when the Bradleys were loaded aboard heavy equipment transporters (HET). The troops donned body armor, were issued ammunition, and boarded buses. They were heading to the border to occupy positions on the Tapline Road running roughly parallel with the Kuwait–Iraq border. The trip required days through heavy traffic. There were rest, refueling, and meal stops at roadside kitchens.

Flooding was a condition few expected to be faced with in the desert. The "general purpose, small" or "hex" tent was widely available. 42in-square wooden cargo pallets were used as tent floors and walkways.

Each battalion was assigned a defensive position. In the featureless, flat desert there were seldom any terrain features on which to dig in. They were merely given a six-digit grid coordinate locatable only by Slugger. This would be their home for weeks or months. Engineers bulldozed a 6–10ft-high sand berm around the site. Sometimes lateral berms were bulldozed and individual U-shaped positions for Bradleys, tanks, and ITVs were built around the perimeter. Beside this would be an attached J-shaped berm in which the crew pitched a tent (or "hootch"). Companies were assigned defense sectors all around. Fighting positions and bunkers may have been built, but mechanized battalions relied on the berm-protected Bradleys and ITVs spotted around the perimeter.

Base camps were divided into a life support area and motor pool. The LSA included the TOC (tactical operations center), sleeping quarters, mess, kitchen, latrines, wash facilities, and other support facilities. Radio antennas were thick on the skyline of each of the bases. All manner of tents were provided including the old canvas GP (General-Purpose), small ("hex") and GP, medium squad tents; newer type vinyl tents, locally purchased white "Bedouin tents", and civilian camping tents purchased by some officers. This led to two standards of living – "bad" with heating stoves, electric lights, and candles permitted in GP tents; and "worse" in the flammable Bedouin tents in which these conveniences were prohibited. Generators provided some power for lighting and a few appliances.

Initially most troops slept on the ground insulated by a ½in. foam pad that offered no cushioning. Flattened corrugated MRE cartons were also used for insulation and the soldier's meager possessions were stowed in a carton under his cot. Folding aluminum cots were later provided owing to the presence of snakes and scorpions, but their taut nylon bed was like sleeping on plywood. Sleeping bags were as much for padding as warmth. Slit trenches, above-ground berms, or sandbag bunkers with overhead cover were built beside each widely separated tent, which were scattered about irregularly. The motor pool area served as the vehicle park, maintenance area, fuel dump, and ammo storage point (ASP).

A promotion, or perhaps the announcement of a new baby at home, or any other occasion for rejoicing called for a much appreciated water dousing from 5-gal cans whilst doing push ups.

Sanitation was a major problem, as was water. A division consumed 120,000 gallons a day and it all had to be trucked in to each camp; two or three water runs were required daily. Water was supplied in water trailers, 5gal plastic cans, and 1.5-liter and smaller plastic bottles. This is partly responsible for the growing popularity of bottled water. Shower stalls and latrines were made of plywood, built by local contractors. Cold showers were the norm, called "Tarzan showers" because of the yells they evoked. Immersion heaters became available to heat shower water. These were originally used to boil water in garbage cans – "GI cans" – to clean mess gear. They were unnecessary for this purpose since Styrofoam and plastic utensils were now used. Washstands using plastic pans were built of 2 x 4s and plastic 5gal water cans were the main source of water. Latrines – "three-hole shitters" – had cut-down 55gal drums. These were pulled out from beneath the seats

Guard posts were conspicuous in the barren desert, no matter how one camouflaged them. Both gray-green and sand-colored sandbags were issued. These troops are wearing their body armor.

once a day, JP-8 fuel (used in all Army vehicles, generators, heaters, and helicopters replacing JP-4, diesel, and gasoline) was stirred in, burned, and the residue buried; it was a most disagreeable job. Units often added screening to keep out flies. A frequent question was, "Where do the flies go at night?" In units other than infantry, latrine and shower doors would be stenciled "Male" and "Female." JP-8 was spread on the sand to keep out scorpions. The pre-fab washstands had taps to be hooked up to waterlines, but this was seldom available. The stands had inset plastic pans and mirrors. Urinals consisted of a 2in-diameter PVC pipe jammed into the sand at an angle with a plastic funnel or bottomless plastic water bottle duct-taped on; they were known as "piss tubes."

Entertainment was limited. Volleyball courts and baseball, football and soccer fields were laid out, their borders marked with the thousands of half-buried empty water bottles, which also marked paths, parade grounds, etc. A "rec tent" was set up usually with a TV and VCR player, and families sent movies that were shared with all. Card games, mainly poker and solitaire, were popular, as were board games. Units accumulated paperback book libraries from those sent from home and *Soldier Magazine*, *Star and Stripes*, *USA Today*, *Arab News*, *Saudi Gazette* (the last two being local English papers) and divisional papers were available.

Military operations on urbanized terrain (MOUT) training being conducted in a desert town. Note the blank firing attachment. The specialist in the foreground wears the desert night camouflage smock issued with the desert BDUs. Its green grid pattern was designed to be difficult to detect with night vision devices.

Conditions were Spartan and there were shortages of everything. So many troops were pouring into Saudi Arabia, and without an established and developed logistics infrastructure, distributing supplies to the units was a patchy process. Thousands of local contractors were hired to move supplies, spare parts, and water and provide services. Workers were brought in from the world over. By December 1990, though, on the eve of the Ground War, supplies were generally plentiful. The Armed Forces Radio and Television Service operated "Shield 107" radio station, broadcasting from Dhahran. Mail call was frequent with letters, "care packages," and "comfort kits" with toilet items and other items addressed to "Any Service Member" from support groups at home.

Brigade-operated PX trucks made the rounds to outlying camps weekly or bi-weekly. Some troops were rotated or sent for details to the Division Support Area where there was a PX, phone center donated by AT&T, shoppette, and Arab gift shops. There was a Rest and Relaxation Center near Dhahran and a Cunard cruise ship docked at Bahrain, but few forward-deployed combat troops saw these. The battalions deployed on the border occasionally saw female soldiers in support units, referred to as BBCs – "bleached blondes in combat" (owing to a shortage of hair dye) – and even more rarely burka-clad Bedouin women, known as BMO – black moving objects, as described by observers seeing them approaching from afar.

An M2 Bradley with the twin TOW launcher swung out in the firing mode. On the right front fender the division designation was on top (1 CAV, 1 IN, 24 IN, 1 AR, 2 AR, 3 AR) and below it was the battalion designation (2-4 CAV or 3-41 IN, for example). On the left fender were the company and the vehicle number within the company, here C 22 – "Charlie Two-Two."

No alcoholic beverages of any kind were permitted out of respect for Islamic culture. There were instances of overreaction in this respect. At one point it was assumed the American flag sewn on uniforms might cause problems, and they were ordered removed. However, they were soon restored, and US flags were hoisted over bases. To the Americans Arab culture was strange, especially since it restricted their own freedoms, such as drinking alcohol. Little effort was made to understand the culture, which was simply too alien for most. While officially discouraged, US troops privately referred to Arabs as "rag-heads," "towel-heads," or "sand niggers." They had little faith in the fighting abilities of their Arab allies and there were even concerns about their being turned against.

The necessity and urgency of the situation allowed for a degree of training seldom achieved in garrison, which saw many distractions owing to the Army's bureaucratic tendencies. Individual skills were honed and teamwork developed. Soldiers knew this was for real and even the reluctant realized it was time to get serious. They cross-trained on weapons and other equipment so that every man in the squad could do another's job.

Chow time

The primary combat ration was the "Meal, Ready-to-Eat, Individual," or MRE. Much has been written about this, most of it unfavorable. The troops referred to them as "meals rejected by Ethiopians" or "meals rejected by everyone." There are limitations to how palatable a ration can be considering the requirements for protective packaging, resistance to temperature extremes, a long shelf life, and for being lightweight, etc. There were complaints of constipation after prolonged use. This was due to the low moisture content. One cannot expect restaurant quality foods from such. Many of

The "dismounts" practice dismounting and deploying for close-in security. The squad SAW gunner is to the left. This was a "green day" when woodland pattern BDUs were worn, and the desert BDUs were washed.

the complaints, though, were simply due to soldiers being used to high-fat content fast foods, preconceived dislike (it's not "real" food), and simply an automatic dislike for anything out of the ordinary. It was not uncommon during short training exercises for troops to stock up on snacks and commercial foods such as beanie weenies and Raman noodles, which had little more going for them than MREs.

Many of the 1981–87 entrées were freeze-dried, and while they could be eaten dry, were better reconstituted with hot water. These were still being issued during the Gulf War. The 1988 issue saw improved non-freeze-dried entrées and they were increased from 5oz to 8oz, a common complaint being that they were not filling. Other improvements were made in components, and a tiny Tabasco sauce bottle was added to some menus, a popular condiment to spice up the flavor. Some entrées were less popular than others – such as the "four fingers of death" (frankfurters and beans) and "wild turkey surprise" (turkey diced with sauce). Meal trading was common. The flameless ration heater, a device creating a chemical reaction, was shipped to the theater, but distribution problems and the quick end to the war saw few reaching troops. Most soldiers consumed MREs cold, although laying the entrées in the blazing sun on a tent or fender warmed them in 15 minutes.

Distribution varied. Often soldiers just pulled a bag out of a case of 12 at random, or from a set laid on the ground with the label facing down. Any undesired choices might be traded, or they might not. In some units one could pick and choose.

A single meal provided 1,200 calories. Storage life was three years. They were not supposed to be eaten for over 21 days straight. This was extended if some meals were A and B-rations. Efforts were made to provide fruit,

Meals, ready to eat

Menu	1981–87 issue	1988–92 issue
1	Pork patty	Pork w/rice in barbecue sauce
2	Ham and chicken loaf	Corned beef hash
3	Beef patty	Chicken stew
4	Beef slices in barbecue sauce	Omelet w/ham
5	Beef stew	Spaghetti w/meat sauce
6	Frankfurters w/beans	Chicken à la king
7	Turkey diced w/gravy	Beef stew
8	Beef diced w/gravy	Ham slice
9	Chicken à la king	Meatballs w/tomato sauce
10	Meatballs w/barbecue sauce	Tuna w/noodles
11	Ham slice	Chicken w/rice
12	Beef w/spiced sauce	Escalloped potatoes w/ham
13	Chicken loaf	—

Side dish (fruit, rice, corn, mashed potatoes, etc.)

Crackers or bread

Spread (jelly, peanut butter, cheese spread)

Dessert (cookies, cake) or snack candy

Beverage (fruit or sports drink mix, cocoa, coffee, tea)

Tabasco sauce (in some)

Accessory pack (matches, dry creamer, sugar, salt, pepper, chewing gum, toilet paper)

Plastic spoon

The rifle companies were supported by the battalion's six 4.2in M106A3 mortar carriers, a modified M113A3 APC. Just below the open mortar hatch can be seen the mortar's base plate, which allowed it to be dismounted for firing if necessary.

snacks, and drinks to supplement MREs. It was not uncommon in the field, training or deployed, for hot breakfasts and dinners to be served with an MRE lunch. The Army made efforts to provide as many fresh food meals as possible. Fifty percent of the rations shipped into the theater were MREs, 91 million meals. Some 24 million commercially packaged meals were issued such as Dinty Moore and Lunch Buckets.

A-rations were locally purchased fresh foods. B-rations were canned, dehydrated, and other preserved foods similar to A-rations, but which did not require refrigeration. Many of them were provided in No. 10 (1gal) cans with items such as powdered eggs and mashed potatoes; premixed pancake, waffle, biscuit and cake mixes; and canned fruits and vegetables as well as canned meats.

B-rations were still in use, but a new field feeding system was available, the T-ration or tray-pack. These were aluminum trays providing 36 portions of pre-cooked food such as beef pot roast, lasagna, casseroles, vegetables, desserts, etc. There were 10 each T-ration breakfast and lunch/dinner menus providing 54 different dishes. One complaint was the limited number of breakfast foods. Paper and plastic plates, cups, and utensils were provided with T-rations. T-rations were prepared and served from the mobile kitchen trailer (MKT) optimistically operated by a single cook assisted by KPs. The MKT was inadequate for the job lacking interior lighting, plumbing, ventilation, and water storage. A serious problem was the amount of time required to heat up the stove and oven. A single cook with untrained assistance was incapable of providing two, much less three, meals a day. The Army's limited stock of T-rations soon ran out.

The excessive packaging of every MRE component created a considerable pile of plastic, Mylar, and paper, a common complaint. Directives prohibited simply discarding trash or even burying it. It was to be collected in plastic trash bags and burned daily.

Regardless of the food, eating in the desert was a challenging proposition. Sand and dust found its way into food and drinks. Dust worked its way into clothes, sleeping bags, radios, and weapons. By the time they got to troops, "hot" meals were no longer so. The insistent heat coupled with hard work and training exercises made it sometimes difficult to eat. Water was occasionally in short supply and hot drinking water was less than pleasant. Biting flies were a constant annoyance as were poisonous snakes, scorpions, and massive camel spiders. After months in the desert rumors began to circulate of six or 12-month rotations, or even of the move becoming a permanent change of station.

"Dismounts" rush out of their Bradley and immediately spread out. The Bradley crew would be providing covering fire with the 25mm gun and 7.62mm machine gun.

THE SOLDIER IN BATTLE

In a light dust storm a squad leader gives directions to his men; most have their goggles over their eyes. Training continued regardless of the weather, as combat would not cease regardless of how bad conditions became.

The goal of the Air War was to destroy at least 50 percent of the Iraqi combat capabilities, with the focus on AFVs, artillery, and air defense. Particular attention was given to Republican Guard units. By the end of 1990 Saddam had 530,000 troops, 4,000 tanks, and 3,000 guns facing the Coalition. Saddam's "Mother of All Battles" was nearing. Troops stood on perimeter berms at night, cheering the spectacle of air and artillery strikes.

Engineers built replicas of the Iraqi battalion defensive positions in the rear: large triangular sand forts with company positions in each corner and protected by minefields, barbed wire, and the "dreaded" fire trenches. The latter were trenches filled with abundant crude oil to be ignited when the Americans approached. The media naively made much of these "formidable" obstacles. Many were simply pre-ignited by artillery fire; to overcome them, engineers bulldozed 20ft-wide sand causeways across. In live-fire exercises, trench complexes were dug and troops assaulted them. Shooting houses were constructed out of stacked sand-filled tires in which to practice clearing buildings, and vast ranges constructed for all weapons. NBC training exercises were frequent.

All MOPP-ed up

"Mission-Oriented Protective Posture" describes five levels of clothing and equipment for protection from nuclear, biological, and chemical (NBC) threats. MOPP zero is the normal field uniform with the protective mask carried and

E **DESERT STORM MECHANIZED INFANTRYMAN**
The desert BDUs were issued to most of the troops deploying from the States (**1**), the five-color "chocolate chip" uniform. Most troops carried a second 1-qt canteen and a small M1961 combat pack or "butt pack." This infantryman wears the ill-suited jungle boots with black canvas uppers. A desert hat and sunglasses, usually frowned on, are worn here. Figure **2** has donned full "MOPP" or MOPP 4. The suits were issued in both olive drab and woodland camouflage pattern. The gloves are of heavy black rubber, worn over thin white cotton gloves to make them more comfortable. The "one-size-fits-all" chemical protection boots were commonly known as "elf boots" owing to their turned-up toes when laced. All troops carried an M258A1 decontamination kit (**10**) containing three cleansing wipes and three additional chemical neutralizing wipes, which were activated by snapping enclosed glass ampules. Soldiers carried two atropine auto-injectors (**11**) for nerve agent antidote. They were activated by removing the cap and slapping the (larger) injector onto the thigh to automatically inject it. If symptoms persisted after 10 minutes the second (smaller) set was injected. Soldiers also carried a booklet of M8 detection paper (**3**). If touched against suspect droplets, its color would change thus identifying the chemical agent. Stripes of M9 detection tape from a dispenser (**4**) were fastened around the right upper arm, lower left arm, and lower left leg on the MOPP suit. The Meal, Ready-to-Eat (**5**) was provided in dark brown packets at the time. Twelve MREs were issued in a case (**6**), these were often seen strapped to vehicles wherever there was space. The Gulf War was the first conflict in which wide use was made of the Global Positioning System (GPS) for weapon targeting and navigation. Units were quickly issued AN/PSN-10 Small Lightweight GPS Receivers (SLGR – "Slugger") (**8**). The MX-991/U flashlight (**9**) was standard issue, but many small civilian flashlights were used. Blue-green filters had replaced the red as a better means of preserving night vision and limiting the revealing glare. Two-quart canteens (**12**) were soon issued to all field troops in addition to their 1-quarts. The old olive green versions were also issued. Also shown is an M67 frag grenade (**7**).

A squad grenadier armed with an M16A2 rifle and M203 grenade launcher. Grenadiers carried at least eighteen 40mm rounds.

the NBC protective suit, gloves, and overboots readily available. MOPP 1 saw the suit worn and the mask, gloves, and boots, carried. MOPP 2 was the same, but the boots were worn. MOPP 3 saw the suit, mask, and boots worn and the gloves carried. MOPP 4 was with all items donned. Under MOPP 1 through 3 the coat and mask's hood could be left open for ventilation in hot weather. The prescribed MOPP level depended on a unit's proximity to enemy positions and the enemy's assessed capabilities. The olive drab or woodland pattern coat and trousers of the protective overgarment – the "MOPP suit" – was lined with charcoal-impregnated polyurethane foam. This outfit did not "breathe" and even a few minutes of exertion in hot weather caused excessive sweating. In 20 minutes a man and all garments would be thoroughly drenched in sweat. The suit became ineffective if soaked by sweat or rain. Under ideal conditions it provided up to six hours' protection. A couple of hours wearing MOPP gear could result in heat exhaustion and dehydration. It restricted movement, vision, and hearing and lengthened the time to accomplish even simple tasks. It was not something the troops liked much. As winter set in and MOPP 3 was the rule when the border was crossed, there were few complaints about its added warmth, but it did have to be kept dry.

The threat of chemical and biological attack was a very real concern. The Army had long prepared for such attacks from the Soviets. Detection, protection, and decontamination equipment were abundant and the troops had long trained for it. The Iraqis had used chemical weapons on the Iranians and their own Kurds. They possessed the capabilities and the will. The Iraqis could deliver chemicals by artillery, multiple rocket launchers, aerial bombs, and Scud missiles. The troops took additional NBC training seriously. Regardless, it was much disliked for its discomfort, repetition, and ominous implications.

The 100-hour Ground War

Rumors preceded the actual launch of the Ground War. Various feints, probes, reconnaissance-in-force thrusts, artillery raids, and deception operations had been directed across the border. These were to test Iraqi defenses and capabilities, further cripple them, cover the repositioning of Coalition forces, and build Coalition morale while degrading that of the enemy.

A combat engineer (a platoon or squad of these might be attached to a mechanized battalion) uses an AN/PPS-12 mine detector. Mines proved to be a greater threat than Iraqi antiarmor weapons. In the background to the left other troops are lifting detected mines.

These proved to be false starts for the excited troops finally anticipating action. Artillery and air strikes were increasing. More helicopters were seen and there was a lot of activity in the TOC. The troops felt action was nearing. There was little left to do. They were cocked and ready. Fuel tanks were topped off, commo checks were made over the radios, water cans and canteens filled, and MREs shoved into empty spaces on Bradleys. Few missed the chaplain's rounds.

Company COs were called to the TOC and before long returned giving "thumbs up" signs, and called for the orders group – XO, platoon leaders, and first sergeant. Squads and crews stood around or huddled in their tracks. The desert winter had brought cold and rain. The talcum powder-like dust turned to paste, then mud. The north wind blew Coalition safe conduct passes from across the border. Trucks stuck in patches of ground that

A "tanker truck" driver hands a fuel hose up to a Bradley crewman at a Refuel on the Move (ROM) point, where a company of 13 Bradleys could be refueled in 15 minutes.

Infantrymen search an abandoned Iraqi bunker recovering weapons, munitions, anything of intelligence value, and souvenirs. Weapons could not be brought back as war trophies, but uniforms, insignia, web gear, and similar harmless items were permitted as souvenirs.

previously were firm. MOPP 3 was ordered. It was a long night with an endless display of fireworks across the border. At one point three MLRSs rolled up some distance away and within minutes of arriving each let loose 12 blazing rockets. Just as quickly the vehicles darted off to their reload sites, even before the rockets began air-bursting over Iraqi positions showering them with hundreds of bomblets.

Before dawn they were ordered to deploy. In often-practiced moves they formed up and rolled out of the camp toward their tactical assembly area. They drove under radio silence and blackout conditions using night vision gear. The attached tank company fanned out ahead taking up firing positions. Companies A and B formed up in diamond formations behind the tanks. The TOW company took up over-watching positions to the rear and the mortars were set up to fire smoke shells to cover their advance. Further to the rear first sergeants lined up the support vehicles. (Company D had been exchanged for the tank company.)

They knew combat engineers were forward of the tanks and approaching the Berm, a broad 10–15ft wall of sand running the entire length of the border on the Saudi side. There was concern about crossing over this first obstacle. With the sun rising, hopefully to interfere with Iraqi target acquisition, Bradleys and Abrams would be silhouetted as they crossed over. The piled loose sand could bog down a tracked vehicle. Engineers had previously crept forward and emplaced cratering charges to blow gaps. Armored vehicle-launched bridges would lay 60ft scissor bridges over the Berm and antitank ditches. Trailer-mounted mine-clearing line charge projectors were emplaced to rocket-propel 350ft-long, linear, 1,750-lb demolition charges to blast five meter-wide gaps. Armored engineer combat vehicles with 165mm demolition guns were prepared to blast and bulldoze gaps through obstacles. Engineers stood by with mine detectors and obstacle destroying demolition charges.

Squads were jammed inside their Bradleys with little elbow room among the weapons, ammo, rations, radio batteries, and gear. Wearing helmets, body armor, MOPP suits, rain jackets, web gear, and holding weapons they may have been warm, but they felt constrained. They bore the concerns of all soldiers before them of the apprehension and uncertainty of combat, the first real action for just about every one of them. How would they perform? They feared letting down their buddies with whom they had trained, prepared, and shared the trials of desert life for so long.

Before dawn on January 24, 1991 – G-Day – flashlight signals were passed between tracks. Bradley Commanders (BC) simply said, "Heads up guys," or "We're good to go," or "It's showtime," and the idling engines revved up and they edged forward. Apache attack helicopters passed on a flank. The still darkened sky ahead of them was continuously lit by rippling flashes. Chemical light sticks marked 30ft gaps in the Berm and minefield lanes. Some units had to top the Berm and dashed across at maximum speed and down the other side.

Shattering breaching explosions detonated in front of them as the engineers cleared the way. Artillery barrages blasted across the skyline. Fighter-bombers and attack helicopters were seen only from afar, being kept at a distance to prevent "blue-on-blue" fire incidents – a great fear at all command echelons. Radios were on now, but chatter was minimal, reporting only essential observations and directions given to increase intervals, close them up, or hold their position information.

Troops wearing M17A2 protective masks and desert night camouflage smocks cut through barbed wire. They wear black field or tan leather work gloves, as opposed to rubber chemical protective gloves.

They rolled into Iraq with massed artillery blasting a path before them. They felt they were in the forefront of the attack, but then they funneled into marked lanes through minefields, gaps plowed through wire entanglements, and over bulldozed causeways bridging blackened, burned-out fire trenches. There was a thick oily smell. As the sky lightened the smell's source was revealed. Massive pitch black columns of burning oil were dotted across the horizon. Saddam had ordered thousands of Kuwaiti oil wells to be ignited.

Inside the Bradleys the infantrymen could see little, even through the narrow vision of the firing port periscopes. Both the BC and gunner simultaneously used the integrated sight unit to detect targets, aim, and fire the turret weapons. The thermal imaging night sight could be used day or night to see through smoke, dust, and rain. The BC also had all-around vision with a day and night vision periscope plus a hatch that could be cracked open for unobstructed vision, but which was still protected from overhead shell bursts. The turret crew kept the squad members appraised as best they could. There would be periods of relatively smooth steady cruising, then rough jolting, jostling the troops. There would be starts and stops, brief halts, and then suddenly they darted ahead to the high-pitched whining of the diesel engine. The pitch also increased as they plowed through softer sand.

Occasional rounds of poorly calculated Iraqi artillery fell, usually behind the formation or to a flank. The crews either abandoned their guns or were obliterated within minutes by US counterfire. Their own tanks would suddenly bang off rounds at unseen targets making kills at over 3,000m, far beyond the expected practical range. Detecting T-72 heat signatures, American tanks were shooting SABOT rounds through sand berms and knocking them out. Iraqi tankers were dying before they could even detect the advancing Americans.

Mechanized infantrymen of the 1st Brigade, 2d Armored Division ("Tiger Brigade") cover the Al-Mutia police station, where a vicious room-to-room battle developed.

Where were the massed artillery barrage, tank counterattacks, salvos of antitank missiles, and chemical attacks? The company was approaching a sand fort. Engineer M113s had hooked tow cables to wire entanglements and simply driven away, uprooting hundreds of feet of wire and pickets. 155mm artillery rounds were air-bursting over the fort, from which columns of black smoke boiled. 25mm and machine-gun fire racked the berm. There was no return fire and the tracks rolled up to the berm using it as cover. The BC gave the dismounts a brief description of the surrounding ground to orient them. The squad leader directed which way to maneuver. Admonished to "Be careful out there, guys," the rear ramp was dropped and men were bounding out before it touched the ground.

Taking a few seconds to orient themselves, the platoon dismounts formed up following their fire team leaders. Team leaders led by example – "Follow me; do as I do." Scouts went over the berm and found devastation. The dismounts fanned out and worked their way through the wreckage and gutted vehicle hulks. There were horribly mutilated and burned bodies scattered throughout. The real threat became apparent. There were occasional dud 155mm projectiles and numerous unexploded MLRS bomblets scattered about. Checking in bunkers they found radios, maps, and stacks of documents. Orders came down to leave everything in place for fear of booby traps and collecting souvenirs was forbidden. Intelligence and EOD specialists would sift through the bunkers to collect intelligence information. Behind the fort they found scores of unmarked graves.

CASE/16

MALE
COMFORT KIT
CASE/16

MALE
COMFORT KIT
CASE/16

MALE
COMFORT KIT
CASE/16

For those waiting to return home, the time was passed reading, writing letters, napping, playing cards, or simply "shooting the bull" with buddies. Male comfort kits contained a toothbrush, toothpaste, razor, shaving cream, soap, foot powder, tissues, shampoo, deodorant stick, lip balm, hygiene wipe, sunscreen, toilet paper, eye drops, and laundry detergent.

Their Bradleys met them on the far side of the fort. They quickly re-boarded and moved on, passing burned-out trucks and dozens of artillery positions, their blackened barrels still elevated. Vehicles, bodies, and craters covered the ground around the gun pits. Impossible amounts of paper blew across the ground with a haze of black smoke from the well fires.

Radios crackled and turrets sung to the right front. Movement had been detected among some burned-out trucks and buses. The BC shouted down to the expectant squad, "Iraqi soldiers are coming out. They're surrendering!" It was true. Several dozen Iraqis were meekly walking toward the Bradleys, their hands held high, clutching safe conduct passes. It was raining again. The prisoners had discarded their weapons and equipment; some lacked boots. They begged for food and water. The Iraqis looked filthy, sick, dehydrated, and cold. Unprepared for large numbers of surrendering soldiers, they merely directed the shocked (but grateful to be alive) prisoners to the rear. MPs collected them, and were even forced to seek the help of service units to manage the mass of prisoners.

The battalion task force continued to advance. A ragged artillery barrage impacted near the unit's right flank. Intervals were widened and the speed increased to move out of the area. No devastating barrage struck, however. This occurred several times as the Iraqis were firing and then running away. Tankers reported that once they opened fire on Iraqi tanks the crews sometimes immediately abandoned them.

Ahead there was a bang, and a Bradley was engulfed in a gray cloud. It had hit a mine and two men were wounded. The first sergeant's M113 arrived within minutes, immediately followed by medics. The company continued to advance. Mortar rounds fell among the formation. They had no effect and the Bradleys fanned out in an attack formation. The crackle of machine-gun fire could be heard. The battalion's own 4.2in mortars began slamming rounds into a trench system up ahead.

Abrams maneuvered to the left flank of the enemy position and began pumping rounds into it. Only light small-arms fire was returned and an occasional RPG-7 rocket whizzed past. The Bradleys opened up with 25mm and machine guns peppering the trenches. Red tracers bounced into the sky. Some Iraqis could be seen running, both to the rear and toward the Americans with their hands up. Here the first hardcore holdouts were encountered. Bradleys straddled the trenches cleaning them out with 25mm, machine guns, and FPWs. Tanks rolled to a stop atop bunkers and pivot turned crushing them. Tank companies had one or two dozer tanks and they did not hesitate to run the blade down trenches plowing them under. The infantrymen did not even have to dismount as the position was overrun and resistance literally crushed. It was horrible carnage, but the Iraqis were given ample opportunity to surrender.

The infantry began to feel like they were along for the ride, not that many were complaining about not having to expose themselves. They knew full well at any minute they might have to dismount or be taken under antitank fire. Their derision toward the Iraqis grew steadily.

Suddenly the Bradley jolted to a halt rocking forward. Firing orders were heard from the turret.

"BTR, three o'clock!" The turret skewed to the right.

The gunner shouted, "Identified!" The TOW launcher servo-motors could be heard.

"Fire!" the BC shouted.

The gunner screamed, "On the way!" followed by a bang and a whoosh.

Long seconds passed and a muffled thump was heard followed by cheers from the turret crew, taken up by the dismounts.

The Bradley lurched ahead and the gunner shouted down that they had just blown apart a BTR-60, a Soviet-built eight-wheel APC armed with a 14.5mm machine gun. Troops on the right side of the compartment jostled to take a look out the periscopes at the burning hulk.

Night fell. The unit kept moving through the darkness with infrequent halts. Artillery seemed to be firing somewhere perpetually. A sandstorm mixed with rain began early on the 26th. Visibility was non-existent.

Companies rolled into Refuel on the Move (ROM) points where dozens of fuel tankers were lined up. A crewman jumped off the Bradley, grabbed a hose offered by a support soldier, and stuck it into the filler cap with the engine running. A company refueled in 15 minutes and was off again.

The unit was approaching Kuwait City and infantry were dismounting to clear scattered buildings along roads. There was occasional sniper fire, and another company fought a short battle at a police station. They killed a dozen Iraqis and suffered only two wounded.

They continued to move, and soon ceasefire rumors came over the radio. Hundreds of Iraqi soldiers were surrendering, stumbling out of buildings and coming down roads. They all wanted water. Before dusk they were ordered to take up defensive positions and be prepared to continue the attack at dawn. Republican Guard units were reported to be dug in ahead. At 0800 hours on the 27th the ceasefire was ordered. They had traveled some 300km, with barely a breakdown and only three wounded in their company.

THE AFTERMATH OF BATTLE

It was over. After long months of preparatory work and boredom the Ground War had lasted a mere 100 hours. There were still weeks and even months of sitting on the border watching the Iraqis, escorting convoys, and cleaning up the battlefield. Units began to be rotated home in mid-March, the longest deployed going first.

US Army casualties totaled 98 killed in action, 126 non-hostile deaths, and 354 wounded in action out of 271,654 in the theater. Unfortunately almost a third of the combat casualties were caused by friendly fire owing to night actions and poor visibility. A total of nine Bradleys and M113s were lost. Some estimates state that 100,000 Iraqi troops were killed, although the figures were probably not that high, plus 60,000 POWs.

When the much-anticipated word arrived to redeploy, a great deal of work was necessary. It was deployment in reverse. Vehicles and equipment had to be cleaned, repaired, and readied for shipment. There were the usual schedule and date changes and finally they had a solid departure date after long boring waits in warehouses. The flight home was not fast enough for most. The troops were loaded with gifts in anticipation of the homecoming. The military posts were nearly ghost towns and the adjacent communities had suffered financially with the absence of thousands of soldiers and their dependents. It was more than just the families who welcomed back their soldiers. Yellow ribbons adorned every light post and telephone pole, and magnetic ribbons were seen on countless cars.

Units arrived at a nearby Air Force base and were bused to post gymnasiums or hangars where expectant families waited. Companies or whole battalions formed up, often removing their headgear so they would be recognizable, and with a band playing and their families cheering, they marched in as victors.

The Gulf War was considered a just war by many, and the shabby treatment of troops returning from Vietnam was consciously avoided. An appreciative nation showed its gratitude. As with any other war there were problems. "Gulf War illness/syndrome" emerged, causing various physical problems among some veterans. Its cause has never been determined, but has been attributed to anthrax vaccine, chemical weapons, depleted uranium projectiles, oil well fires, and infectious diseases. The Veterans Administration has taken measures to care for veterans suffering from the illness. This is also the principal goal of the Gulf War Veterans Association.

A large percentage of the Army saw service in the Gulf and it launched the careers of many officers and NCOs. The conflict had a major impact on the development of heavy force tactics, fire support, intelligence collection and dissemination, deployment logistics, and many other areas.

MUSEUMS AND COLLECTIONS

There are no museums dedicated specifically to the Gulf War. The divisional museums of those remaining divisions that fought in the Gulf War maintain displays commentating on their participation. Such displays typically exhibit photographs, uniforms, insignia, individual equipment, weapons, mementoes, and trophies of enemy items. They often possess outdoor displays of Iraqi AFVs and other vehicles, and artillery pieces. Divisional museums include the 1st Cavalry Division – Ft Hood, TX: 1st Infantry Division – Ft Riley, KS; 1st Armored Division – Baumholder, Germany; 3d Infantry Division – Ft Stewart,

GA; 82d Airborne Division – Ft Bragg, NC; and 101st Airborne Division – Ft Campbell, KY. The National Infantry Museum – Ft Benning, GA – and the West Point Museum – West Point, NY – both have Gulf War infantry-related collections. Branch service schools and centers and large Army post museums also have Gulf War-related displays, although they may not be infantry-related.

Home at last. They knew they had done a good job and were rightfully proud of their accomplishments. Now they could sew the patch of the unit they served in during *Desert Storm* on their right shoulder, as a "combat patch."

Collecting

Gulf War uniforms, insignia, equipment, memorabilia, and other items are readily available usually at moderate prices. However, it is very difficult, almost impossible, to determine if items are actually from the Gulf War. Just because an equipment item is sand-colored, a uniform is desert-patterned, or a subdued insignia is sand and brown, does not make it a Gulf War artifact. Vast amounts of desert uniforms and sand-colored equipment were ordered during the war with much of it not delivered until after the war was over. It was issued to units involved with reconstruction and security in the region, to peacekeeping forces in the Sinai, to units tasked with Middle East contingency missions, and to the OPFOR at Ft Irwin, CA. A wise collector would not pay high prices for items declared to be from *Desert Storm*. A suggestion to collectors is that while uniform, insignia, and equipment items are desirable pieces, other items may prove more valuable. Memorabilia, military publications, documents, and similar items could become rare collectors' items in the future. The same applies for the items of the Iraqis and of the Coalition allies.

BIBLIOGRAPHY

Campbell, Geoffrey A., *Life of an American Soldier: The Persian Gulf War*, San Diego, CA: Lucent Books, 2001.

Debay, Yves and Green, Michael, *Operation Desert Shield: US Army Deployment, Prelude to "Desert Storm"*, Hong Kong: Concord Publications, 1991.

Dinackus, Thomas D., *Order of Battle: Allied Ground Forces of Operation Desert Storm*, Central Point, OR: Hellgate Press, 2000.

Dunnigan, James F. and Bay, Austin, *From Shield to Storm: High-Tech Weapons, Military Strategy, and Coalition Warfare in the Persian Gulf*, New York: William Morrow, 1992.

Evans, Anthony A. *Gulf War: Desert Shield and Desert Storm, 1990–1991*, London: Greenhill Books, 2001.

Green, Michael and Brown, James D., *M2/M3 Bradley at War*, Osceola, WI: Zenith Press, 2007.

Jaco, Charles, *The Complete Idiot's Guide to the Gulf War*, Indianapolis, IN: Alpha Books, 2002.

Kassner, Elizabeth, *Desert Storm Journal: A Nurse's Story*, Lincoln Center, MA: Cottage Press, 1993.

Leyden, Andrew, *Gulf War Debriefing Book: An After Action Report*, Central Point, OR: Hellgate Press, 1997.

Paskauskas, Joel B, II. *Desert Garb & Gear: The Equipment of America's Desert Warriors*, Hong Kong: Concord Publications, 1994.

Phillips, Jeffery E. and Gregory, Robyn, *America's First Team in the Gulf*, Dallas: Taylor Publishing, 1992.

Rottman, Gordon, Sherman, Steve, and Summers, Scott, *The Official Lite History (and Cookbook) of the Gulf War*, Houston: Electric Strawberry Press, 1991 (RADIX Press, 11715 Bandlon Dr, Houston, TX 77072 – www.specialforcesbooks.com).

ABBREVIATIONS

APC	armored personnel carrier (M113)
AT4	M136 light antiarmor weapon
BC	Bradley commander
BDU	Battledress uniform
BFV	Bradley fighting vehicle (M2 and M3 Bradley)
CO	commanding officer
CP	command post
DBDU	desert battledress uniform
EPW	enemy prisoner of war
HEAT	high-explosive antitank
HMMWV	high-mobility multiple-purpose wheeled vehicle (a.k.a. Humvee, Hummer)
IFV	infantry fighting vehicle (M2 Bradley)
ITV	improved TOW vehicle (M901)
MOPP	mission-oriented protective posture
MRE	meal, ready-to-eat
NBC	nuclear, biological, chemical
NCO	non-commissioned officer
RPG-7	"rocket-propelled grenade"
SAW	squad automatic weapon (M249)
TOC	tactical operations center
TOW	tube-launched, optically tracked, wire-command link guided missile
XO	executive officer

INDEX

References to illustrations are shown in **bold**.